CREATING BRAIN-FRIENDLY CLASSROOMS

Practical Instructional Strategies for Educators

Lowell W. Biller

A SCARECROWEDUCATION BOOK

The Scarecrow Press, Inc.
Lanham, Maryland, and Oxford
2003

A SCARECROWEDUCATION BOOK

Published in the United States of America
by Scarecrow Press, Inc.
A Member of the Rowman & Littlefield Publishing Group
4720 Boston Way, Lanham, Maryland 20706
www.scarecroweducation.com

PO Box 317
Oxford
OX2 9RU, UK

British Library Cataloguing in Publication Information Available

Library of Congress Cataloging-in-Publication Data

Biller, Lowell W., 1957–
  Creating brain-friendly classrooms : practical instructional strategies for
educators / Lowell W. Biller
      p. cm.
"A ScarecrowEducation book."
Includes bibliographical references (p.   ) and index.
  ISBN 0-8108-4612-8 (pbk. : alk. paper)
  1. Teaching. 2. Learning—Physiological aspects. 3. Brain—Localization of
functions. I. Title.
LB1027 .B499 2003
371.102—dc21

                                                        2002012987

∞™ The paper used in this publication meets the minimum requirements of
American National Standard for Information Sciences—Permanence of Paper
for Printed Library Materials, ANSI/NISO Z39.48-1992.
Manufactured in the United States of America.

This book is dedicated to the more than three million K–12 teachers and administrators who have the opportunity to nurture brain-friendly learning; one student at a time.

CONTENTS

ACKNOWLEDGMENTS

There is not adequate space to acknowledge and "thank" all of the people who helped to make this book possible. However, I would like to mention a few very special individuals who unselfishly provided countless hours of support, advice, and professional expertise to this project.

First, I would like to thank Dr. Mark Goldberg, author of *Exceptional School Leaders*, who encouraged me to write this book and patiently guided me through this endeavor.

Second, Eric and Diane Jensen planted the first seeds of passion regarding brain-friendly learning. They helped to increase my knowledge on this subject through excellent workshops and freely provided assistance and advice throughout the initial stages of this book. Other individuals who shared their professional expertise and research and helped me to develop a better understanding about the human brain include Dr. Ken Smith, Dr. Ron Baisden, Dr. George Koob, Dr. Marian Diamond, Dr. Gayatri Devi, Dr. Jim Messina, Dr. Rallie McAllister, and Dr. Mack Hicks.

In addition, the following friends provided technical assistance, editing, and practical suggestions: Carolyn Greer, Sherry Cox, Karen Reed-Wright,

Charlene Shelton, Mike Ritz, Ryan Wagner, Doug Rabel, Dr. Peggy Rochelle, Cookie Greer, and Sandra McGinnis supplied the creative illustrations—thank you!

And finally, to my wife, Betsy, thank you for your enduring support, patience, and love that you have shown me throughout writing this book, and most importantly, throughout each passing day.

INTRODUCTION

Historically, educators have served as instructional leaders, curriculum specialists, mediators of conflicts, mentors, and they have now been bestowed the dubious honor: Interpreters of Brain Research! A wealth of research conducted over the last ten years has uncovered extraordinary data about how the brain processes, stores, and retrieves information. As educators, we must learn how to apply the best of this research to design brain-friendly environments for our students.

The concept of creating brain-friendly classrooms is not a program to implement or a miraculous panacea to increase academic performance or reduce student discipline problems, Effectively using brain research does, however, give educators a foundation of knowledge that provides instructional tools and strategies that are aligned with the way the brain naturally learns and aid in effective teaching and discipline.

Teachers plan learning activities and instructional strategies on a daily basis that directly impact the development of neural pathways inside the brains of all students in their classrooms; it makes sense for teachers to develop a basic understanding of the human brain and how memories are formed. For decades educators have intuitively designed wonderful lessons for their students, with minimal awareness of the internal workings of the brain. Fortunately, with the advent of sophisticated brain imaging techniques such as Positron Emmision Tomography (PET) scans and Functional Magnetic Resonance Imaging (fMRI) technology, neuroscientists and the medical community have a way to view this complex learning organ.

As you begin reading this book, it's important to know that I am not a neuroscientist or an expert on technical brain research. I have spent my entire professional career in public education working at every K–12 level: elementary, middle school, and high school. My interest in and subsequent passion for brain research and the complexities of learning was sparked by an intense desire to more effectively reach all students. The desire to develop an accurate understanding of the brain has led me through an exciting voyage of professional growth.

An incredible learning opportunity came when a renowned neurosurgeon, Dr. Ken Smith of Wellmont Medical Center, invited me to observe him perform a craniotomy. Talk about a humbling experience: to stand by the neurosurgeon in the operating room and watch as he probed around inside a person's brain! To look through the surgeon's powerful microscope and see a pulsating mass of delicate tissue with arteries and veins intricately intertwined over the surface of the brain, and to know that this small glob of tissue that is so fragile you could cut it with edge of your fingernail is what makes us human. This organ allows us to think; to remember pleasant memories from our childhood; to develop and accomplish goals; and it has the potential to solve the world's most complicated problems or to laugh at the most trivial of jokes.

It's incredible to think educators have an opportunity to influence the development of neural pathways inside the brain of each of our students. If we truly want to help students to learn, we have to develop an understanding about how the brain functions; about how children learn and form memories; and just as important, what inhibits learning. Everything teachers do to prepare lessons and to teach these lessons influences student learning either in a positive way or negative way.

I would like to share a story with you which has analogies throughout this book.

There was a man many years ago by the name of Bobby Leach. On July 25, 1911, he became the first man to sucessfully construct an enclosed vessel and survive going over Niagara Falls. It's hard to believe that anyone could actually survive the incredible intensity and power of the Falls.

After Leach courageously accomplished this remarkable feat, he immediately began to tour the world telling people how he was able to conquer the mammoth waterfall. However, guess how Bobby Leach eventually died? He was walking too rapidly down a flight of stairs and someone had dropped a tiny sliver of an orange peel, he lost his footing, fell and died in the fall.

I believe there is a lesson in this that we can use in our classrooms, because we cannot overlook the little things. It's the little things we do that can distinguish an average lesson from a great lesson. It's the little things we do that can make a difference between a mediocre teacher and a truly master teacher, and it's consistently doing the little things well that can transform a good school into a great school.

> It's doing the little things well that can transform a good school into a great school.

Many of the things discussed in this book might seem small or insignificant; however, these techniques and strategies can truly nurture brain-friendly learning—one student at a time.

A LOOK AHEAD

The purpose of this book is to provide teachers and administrators a concise overview of the human brain and how it learns and to present specific instructional strategies and classroom management techniques that are aligned with current research.

As a result of reading this book, you will be able to:

1. Identify the main anatomical regions of the brain and recognize how they are involved with the dynamic process of learning.
2. Understand how the brain receives, processes, and stores information.
3. Develop practical, brain-friendly, instructional strategies and techniques to integrate into the classroom and school environment.

OUTLINE OF CHAPTERS

In Chapter 1, I will discuss the anatomy of the brain and how this information is relevant to every K–12 setting. Chapters 2 to 5 will present the simple, yet powerful, *I-CAN* method to effectively integrate the concepts of brain-friendly learning into the classroom. *I-CAN* is an acronym for the four components of applying brain research in schools: *I*nstructional climate, *C*erebral engagement, *A*bundant connections, and *N*eural practice. In Chapter 6 I will discuss activities and strategies that can stimulate your brain to keep it vibrant and energized.

We are embarking on a new era in education that has the potential to significantly transform the way we teach. By expanding our professional knowledge base and actively applying new understandings of the brain to the classroom, we can proceed to nurture a brain-friendly learning environment; one student at a time.

1

A LOOK INSIDE THE BRAIN

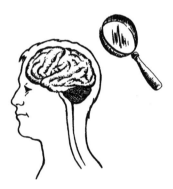

Men ought to know that from nothing else but the brain come joys,
delights, laughter, sorrows, griefs, despondency, and lamentations.

—Hippocrates, *On the Sacred Disease* (fourth century, B.C.)

Your brain is the fundamental essence of who you are as a human being. You can undergo a heart or lung transplant and retain your unique
personality. However, you cannot do this with the brain. Some of the
mysteries of this amazing learning organ are beginning to be uncovered
by neurological research.

One specialized branch of neuroscience is called cognitive neuroscience and is responsible for understanding the neural networks of

intelligence, self-awareness, and how the functions of the brain create the individual mind, the very essence of who we are. Research conducted in this and other areas of neuroscience is beginning to build the knowledge that educators can use to make decisions to help students in the classroom. This journey begins by developing an understanding about the basic composition and anatomical structures of the brain.

COMPOSITION OF THE BRAIN

The adult human brain weighs only about three pounds and is approximately the size of a large grapefruit. Your brain is densely packed and molded to fit inside the skull. If you were to remove the top layer of the brain, the cerebral cortex, and spread it out, it would be approximately the size of a standard newspaper page. A brain this large would make it difficult to pass through the birth canal; therefore, it is tightly compressed to conform to your skull's shape. As a result of being so densely packed inside the cranium, the brain's physical appearance resembles a very large wrinkled, dried-out prune!

The brain is composed primarily of approximately 72 to 78 percent water, 10 to 12 percent protein, and 8 to 10 percent fat. If you were to touch the brain, it would have the consistency of week-old jell-o.

> It is imperative that students drink an adequate supply of water.

Since the brain is made up of so much fluid, it is imperative that students drink an adequate supply of water or they may start feeling mentally sluggish. Lack of water actually impairs the ability to think (Fahey, 2000).

The brain consumes between 20 and 25 percent of your body's total oxygen intake. With every breath you take, approximately 25 percent of it goes directly to your brain. Therefore, it is critical that students move around in the classroom and engage in activities that will increase their oxygen intake. Simply standing up can increase the oxygen

> It is critical that students move around in the classroom and engage in activities that will increase their oxygen intake.

and blood flow to the brain by 15 percent! (Jensen, 1998). The problem with sitting down for long periods of time is that it promotes inadequate breathing patterns, increases fatigue, and adversely impacts the ability to think and learn.

CELLS OF THE BRAIN

All tissues and organs consist of cells and the brain is no exception. The brain consists of two broad categories of cells: neurons and glial cells. The main function of the neurons is to communicate with other neurons to promote our survival. Neurons, of which we have approximately 100 billion, are the most important cells for the distinctive functions of the brain. They are the cells responsible for allowing us to think, communicate, feel, and navigate our bodies throughout our daily routines. The neurons help us to be aware of changes within our environment and to communicate these changes to other neurons in order to alter our body's responses to these sensations. Each neuron works as part of an intricate neural network to facilitate communication within the brain. This process of neuronal communication is accomplished in three distinctly separate and unique steps: receiving a signal or impulse, processing it, and transmitting the signal to other neurons (Drubach, 2000).

The glial cells outnumber neurons by ten to one and serve in a supporting role. The term, glial, is derived from the Greek word meaning "glue," and these cells help to maintain an ideal environment in which our neurons flourish. In the prenatal brain, they provide a structure or support for neurons to grow. As the brain matures, the glial cells function mainly by insulating, protecting, supporting, and nourishing our neurons (Eliot, 1999). Metaphorically, if the brain were a slice of raisin bread, the neurons would represent the raisins and the glial cells would be the bread dough that holds the raisins.

Structure of Neurons

The neurons' purpose of existence is to share information with other neurons in the brain. When this occurs, they flourish and grow; however, if neurons are not stimulated and stop communicating with each other, they can wither and die. The old adage "use it or lose it" is very appropriate when talking about neurons.

To understand how learning takes place, it is important to first be aware of the structure of neurons (see Figure 1.1). Each neuron is composed of a cell body that is referred to as the soma. Within the cell body is a fluid substance called cytoplasm that contributes to the cell's growth, metabolism, and replication. The nucleus, which contains chromosomes, the genetic blueprint for our entire body, is also located in this area of the cell (Drubach, 2000). Other specialized structures within the cell body are ribosomes that use amino acids to make protein for our body and the mitochondria that help to produce energy for the cell body.

Other components of the neuron include multiple projections extending from the top of the cell body, called dendrites. Dendrite is de-

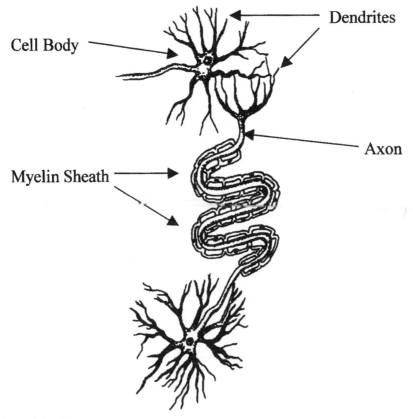

Figure 1.1.   Neuron

rived from the Greek word meaning tree. The dendrites branch out from the cell body to *receive* incoming sensory information from other neurons. They serve as the cell's specialized antennae constantly searching for new signals and sources of information. Once the dendrite receives the new information, it is transferred to the next neuron, through the cell body and down a single nerve fiber called the axon.

The axon, which can measure less than a millimeter to over a meter in length, extends from the bottom of the cell body and is responsible for *sending* electrical impulses to other cells. The axon functions much like a TV cable, transmitting electrical signals in only one direction. In the case of the neuron, the axon only carries the impulses away from the cell body and never toward it. For the electrical messages to be carried in an efficient manner, the axon must be coated with a white, fatty substance called myelin. The purpose of the myelin is to insulate the axon that, in turn, accelerates the communication among the neurons. The myelin is produced by the brain's network of supporting cells called glial.

Glial Cells: The Brain's Internal Army

The brain consists of four different types of glial cells: astrocytes, oligodendrocytes, macrophage, and ependymal.

Astrocytes are the most numerous of the brain's glial cells and have a distinctive star-like appearance. An important function of astrocytes is to maintain a chemical equilibrium in the extracellular space around the neuron, in part, by removing excess neurotransmitters from the synaptic cleft. They also play a critical role in forming the blood-brain barrier to keep toxins from entering the brain.

A second type of glial cell is called oligodendrocytes, and they perform the crucial task of cell myelination.

Macrophage is the third type of glial cell and serves as the brain's primary mode of house cleaning. The macrophages are constantly searching for "dirty" areas of the brain to clean. For example, they remove debris from dead cells and other toxins that may enter the brain.

The fourth glial cell is the ependymal cell. These cells help to form the fluid-filled ventricles within the brain, and they play a pivotal role in directing the migration of neurons during prenatal development by emitting a chemical attractant for the neurons to follow. The ependymal cells also help to form a structure for neurons to grow and expand throughout the six layers of the cerebral cortex (Diamond & Hopson, 1998, Eliot, 1999).

The neurons and glial cells are the molecular structure in which the brain communicates by orchestrating a symphony of electrical impulses and chemical reactions. However, neurotransmitters, peptides, and hormones are the specific substances that trigger the whole process of neuronal communication. When this exchange occurs, the neurons communicate with each other and learning takes place.

THE BRAIN'S INTERNAL MESSENGERS

The communication process begins when dendrites receive information and carry electrical impulses through the cell body and down to the axon's terminal. The neurons do not actually touch one another; therefore, for the message to continue, the electrical impulse must be transformed into a neurotransmitter.

Most neurotransmitters are manufactured within the neurons and are stored in small pockets called *vesicles*. The vesicles are located in the axon terminal and each neurotransmitter has a distinctive physical feature that can only be used by the receiving neuron. When the electrical impulse triggers the vesicles, the neurotransmitter is released into a tiny gap called the synaptic cleft. This transformation from electrical impulse to chemical reaction takes place at the end of the axon terminal of the *sending* neuron and the dendrite of the *receiving* neuron.

The specific neurotransmitter released from the axon has a unique shape that attaches to special openings on the receiving dendrite, called receptors. The neurotransmitter molecules and receptors are similar to a lock and key; each designed only to work with the other (see Figure 1.2). As the receptor site receives the incoming neurotransmitter, the message is once again transformed back into an electrical impulse and the cycle continues until the final destination. Thus, from a classroom perspective, as this process is repeated it forms a neural network and learning is solidified. For example, if students are studying American History and learn that George W. Bush is the 43rd President of the United States, the more this fact is repeated, the more the network of

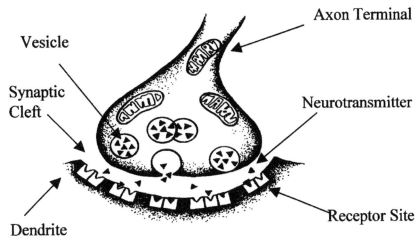

Vesicle

Axon Terminal

Synaptic Cleft

Neurotransmitter

Dendrite

Receptor Site

Figure 1.2. Synapse

neurons responsible for learning this detail will be stimulated and the memory will become stronger.

Neurotransmitters play a crucial role in mediating our emotions, attitudes, and resiliency and they impact how we think and learn. In essence, who we are and what we do is an interaction between and among the chemical messengers within our brains and bodies. Although there may be as many as 100 different neurotransmitters, we will only discuss six that have a significant effect on attention, learning, and memory: acetylcholine, dopamine, endorphin, epinephrine, norepinephrine, and serotonin.

• Acetylcholine was the first neurotransmitter ever discovered. As with most neurotransmitters, it serves several different functions within the brain and body. One of its major roles is communicating with voluntary and involuntary muscles; each time you move, acetylcholine signals your muscles to react. This chemical also plays a key role in slowing down the heart, constricting the pupils of your eyes, enhancing rapid eye movements, and activating the pathways of learning and memory (Hobson, 1999). Without acetylcholine, long-term memories could not be formed.

A great deal of research has implicated the lack of this vital neurotransmitter as a contributing factor of Alzheimer's disease (Gilman & Newman, 1996). There have been some studies that suggest your diet could affect the levels of this chemical in the brain. For example, foods such as egg yolks, liver, peanuts, cauliflower, green leafy vegetables, walnuts, flax seed, and Brazil nuts could increase the amount of acetyl-choline in your body (Carper, 2000; Drubach, 2000).

• Dopamine, like acetylcholine, is used by the brain to perform different functions. It is manufactured deep within the brain in an area called the substantia nigra and has been referred to as the "learning neurotransmitter" (Ratey, 2001). Dopamine has pathways that lead throughout the brain and is responsible for producing pleasurable feelings, maintaining focused attention, and controlling voluntary motor movements.

The constant balance of this neurotransmitter is very important to maintain a normal and happy life. Too much dopamine can result in symptoms of schizophrenia, Tourette's Syndrome, and Obessive-Compulsive Disorder. A deficiency of the dopamine network can contribute to such conditions as Parkinson's disease, depression, and Attention Deficit Disorder (ADD) (Carter, 1998).

The production of dopamine is enhanced when you experience something pleasurable or exciting. It stimulates the neural pathways associated with rewards and helps the brain to remember that the experience was enjoyable and should be repeated. This includes activities such as playing with friends, celebrations, and physical movements like walking or swimming. On the downside, dopamine is also produced during dangerous actions like thrill seeking, taking drugs, and smoking (Jensen, 2000). Dopamine plays an important role in learning, and we will revisit this neurotransmitter throughout this book.

> The production of dopamine is enhanced when you experience something pleasurable or exciting.

• Endorphin, a peptide neurotransmitter, is manufactured in the pituitary gland and helps to alleviate pain and creates a sense of well-being and euphoria. This chemical works in concert with dopamine and serotonin to stimulate the brain's pleasure pathways to produce feelings of satisfaction and contentment. Endorphin levels can be increased in the brain by engaging in such activities as exercise, laughter, pleasurable social interaction, music, and the use of appropriate physical touch (Pert, 1997).

• Epinephrine, also referred to as adrenaline, serves a dual role as a neurotransmitter and hormone. As a hormone, it is produced in the adrenal glands and carried throughout the body in the blood stream. In the brain, epinephrine acts as a neurotransmitter and prepares the body for the fight-or-flight response. It signals the brain to increase the heart rate, stop digestion, constrict blood vessels, and prepare for possible danger. In short bursts, epinephrine can improve memory, enhance attention, and put the brain in an altered state of alert. Conversely, long-term exposure to epinephrine can produce just the opposite effect: memory deficits, difficulty attending to details, and fatigue.

• Norepinephrine, also referred to as noradrenaline, is produced in the sub-cortical brain region called the locus coeruleus. It, too, serves many different roles within the brain and body. This neurotransmitter is involved with maintaining attention and enhancing the formation of memory. Norepinephrine pathways are found throughout the brain and assist in mediating emotional well-being, overall level of alertness, and receptivity to learning. Stimulating and challenging activities can increase the norepinephrine levels in the brain and can lead to improved focus and concentration. In threatening situations, it triggers the adrenal glands to release epinephrine and stimulates the fight-or-flight response.

• Serotonin is manufactured in an area of the brain called the raphe nucleus and plays an essential role in elevating emotions and self-esteem. It has been referred to as the "good mood messenger" because it is associated with optimism and tranquility. Serotonin seems to modulate emotional responses by producing a calming influence on the brain. It impacts virtually every aspect of your life by affecting your mood, memory, energy level, sleep, and overall outlook on life.

> Serotonin has been referred to as the "good mood messenger" because it is associated with optimism and tranquility.

Individuals with low levels of serotonin are vulnerable to alcoholism, depression, low self-esteem, impulsive acts, eating disorders, and suicide (Carper, 2000). People with high levels of serotonin are typically energetic, optimistic, and have a "can do" attitude toward life. A warm smile or friendly pat on the back can increase the production of serotonin, thus serving as a mood enhancer and a positive motivator.

As we have discussed, neurotransmitters play a vital role in how we feel and learn. When all is well, they work synergistically to help you perform and feel your best; however, if neurotransmitters are out of balance, they can have a devastating impact on your brain and body.

A LOOK INSIDE THE BRAIN'S ANATOMY

Our journey inside the brain will begin at the base of the skull and extend to the uppermost regions of the frontal cortex that are inextricably linked to the dynamics of learning and memory. As we briefly move through the brain, we will see how each anatomical region plays a special role in the learning process. The first stop is the cerebellum.

Cerebellum

The cerebellum, Latin for "little brain," is located at the base of the skull (see Figure 1.3) and coordinates virtually all neurological activity (R. Baisden, personal communication, July 2000).

Much of what the brain does is orchestrated by the cerebellum. It is responsible for maintaining the body's equilibrium, muscle tone, and synchronization of voluntary physical movements, and it appears to play a pivotal role in the formation of certain types of memories.

> Much of what the brain does is orchestrated by the cerebellum.

The cerebellum can be compared to a conductor of an enormous symphony orchestra who skillfully monitors and adjusts the musicians' tempo and rhythm to make certain each note is perceived as a fluid, pleasurable tone to the audience's ear. For instance, the cerebellum ensures that our physical movements are performed in a smooth and accurate manner. Here is a simple demonstration. Sit down in a comfortable chair, relax, close your eyes, and place both hands on your thighs. Next, slowly lift your left index finger to your chin and then back to the thigh.

This effortless exercise literally took millions and millions of neurons and muscle cells working synergistically to perform the movements correctly. The part of the brain responsible for coordinating these intricate movements is the cerebellum. Just like the conductor who is astutely aware of each note played in the symphony orchestra, the cerebellum synchronizes millions, if not billions, of individual neurons and muscle cells to "fire" at precisely the correct time to make these movements possible.

The cerebellum is also the part of the brain that appears to store "how to" memories. For example, memories such as how to eat using a spoon or

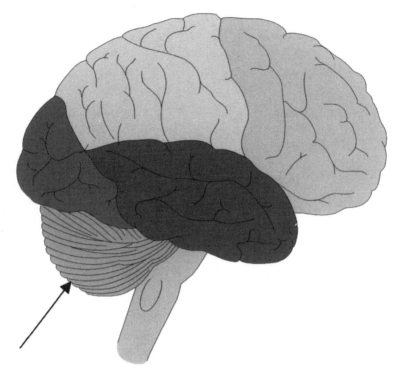

Figure 1.3. Cerebellum

fork, how to swing a golf club, or how to brush your teeth are all controlled by this area of the brain. It is also highly involved with automatic skills associated with reading and the performance of multiplication facts as well as other perfunctory activities like shaking hands or swatting a mosquito that lands on your arm.

> The cerebellum is also the part of the brain that appears to store "how to" memories.

Neuroscientists at Johns Hopkins recently discovered if you are learning a new skill or activity that involves the cerebellum, it takes approximately five to six hours to convert the new learning from short-term memory in the pre-frontal cortex to areas of the brain responsible for the formation

> It takes approximately five to six hours to convert new learning from short-term memory to areas of the brain responsible for permanent motor skills.

of permanent motor skills: the motor cortex, the posterior parietal cortex, and the cerebellum (Ratey, 2001). If a similar task is introduced within this critical period of learning, the retention of the original task could be significantly impaired or even lost. Future research could have real implications for the classroom and could change the way specific skills and activities are taught. We will continue to explore this part of the brain again in Chapter 3 and discuss specific instructional strategies that can stimulate the cerebellum in the classroom. Our journey continues with the centermost regions of the brain: the thalamus, hypothalamus, and pineal gland.

The thalamus, which gets its name from the Greek word for "inner chamber," is nestled deep within the brain. To gauge the approximate location of the thalamus, place your left index finger directly on top of your left ear lobe and place your right index finger on the bridge of your nose. The intersection created by the imaginary lines of your index fingers is the position of the walnut-sized thalamus.

The thalamus is an extremely complex structure that performs numerous vital functions. This anatomical region of the brain is frequently referred to as the "gateway" to the cerebral cortex because all incoming sensory information, with the exception of the olfactory system, is first processed in the thalamus (Gilman & Newman, 1996). As sensory information comes into the brain, the thalamus attempts to organize, categorize, and finally transfer the incoming information to the appropriate areas of the cerebral cortex (Gertz, 1999). Therefore, the thalamus serves as a critical junction for information coming into the brain from the outside world before it is relayed via neural pathways to other areas of the brain. One of these locations is a small, but vitally important network of densely packed neurons called the hypothalamus.

The hypothalamus, as its name suggests, is located directly below the thalamus and regulates many primitive functions of the brain. The hypothalamus aids in controlling the autonomic nervous system, which regulates homeostasis. Homeostasis refers to the body's ability to maintain an internal environment by adjusting our temperature and energy level and monitoring our levels of hydration.

For example, if you become too cold, the hypothalamus will signal your blood flow to be diverted away from the body's surface and the muscles to shiver, thus producing internal heat. If the body becomes too hot, the hypothalamus accelerates the rate of perspiration and your temperature returns to a level of homeostasis. The hypothalamus regulates your appetite and sex drive, and triggers the fight-or-flight response (which we will discuss in more detail in Chapter 2). It also works in concert with the pineal gland to control your sleeping patterns (Mesulam, 2000).

The pineal gland lies in close proximity to the hypothalamus and plays a key role in regulating sleep by releasing a specific hormone. As the brain perceives darkness, it signals the pineal gland to start producing melatonin, which, in turn, encourages the body to start feeling drowsy (Howard, 2000). When this natural, biological process occurs in school, it can result in adverse effects on academic performance. In Chapter 2, we'll investigate the implications that, for instance, a poorly lit classroom can have on student achievement. Now consider the outermost layers of the cerebral cortex and discover the occipital, temporal, parietal, and frontal lobes.

Occipital Lobes

The occipital lobes (see Figure 1.4) are located at the base of the cerebrum and lie just under the skull's occipital bone. This is the area of the brain where vision and visual interpretation are processed. It is where the initial phase of reading begins, and visual memories appear to be stored here. Each neural network in the occipital lobe processes one aspect of vision such as horizontal or vertical lines, color, depth perception, and motion. Each cortical region of the occipital lobe has only one primary responsibility, so the brain must assimilate the incoming visual sensory information into a coherent image that we recognize.

The brain begins the process of sight and visual perception as images from the retina of each eye are channeled via the optic nerve to a small pair of neural structures located on the thalamus called the lateral geniculate nucleus (Zeki, 1999). The lateral geniculate nucleus (LGN) is the "gateway" to the visual cortex and serves as a visual filter for incoming sensory information while mediating our conscious visual perception. At this point, visual information is transferred to the primary visual cortex in the occipital lobe.

For example, if you are walking in a park and suddenly see a small furry animal with sharp teeth and a wagging tail approaching you, the

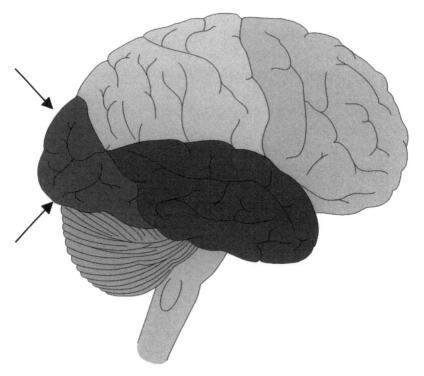

Figure 1.4.   Occipital Lobe

brain will instantly transfer the sensory information from the LGN to the primary visual cortex and begin to sort the incoming stimulus to the visual association areas. This is where the brain begins to integrate and compare the information with previous learning to determine if the image is recognizable. It registers an emotional response to decide if there is an immediate threat, and the brain seeks to find a name for this small furry creature: dog.

Once the brain successfully matches the incoming visual information with a name and your previous experiences, the image becomes relevant and meaningful. If you have had pleasurable experiences in the past with dogs, you will probably reach down and pat it on the head; however, you may react defensively if you have encountered negative associations with dogs in the past. In Chapter 4, we will discuss how you can "prime" the occipital lobes to prepare your students for new learning. Next our journey takes us to a fascinating region located just behind your ears: the temporal lobes.

Temporal Lobes

The temporal lobes are found on the lateral side of your skull just under the temporal bone (see Figure 1.5). This vast area of the brain begins near the temples and extends all the way to the occipital lobes. The temporal lobes have many functions and are divided into specific neuronal clusters that give us our abilities to produce and understand intelligible speech, recognize objects and faces, and recall long-term cognitive memories (Damasio, 1999). In addition, this region is where the auditory cortex is found along with areas that play a key role in learning and the modulation of emotions.

Research has consistently revealed that language is predominantly found in the left hemisphere for approximately 90 percent of the population (Obler & Gjerlow, 1999). Researchers have used fMRI and PET scans to identify sites in the cortex that control aspects of language as specific as centers for naming regular and irregular verbs, naming living things, and the articulation of proper nouns (Ratey, 2001).

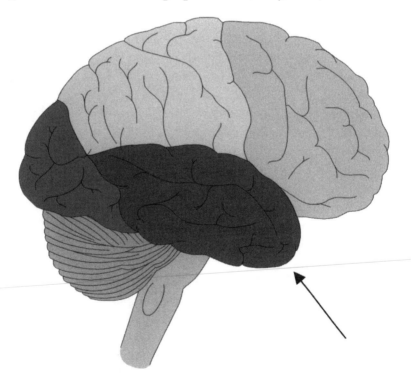

Figure 1.5.   Temporal Lobe

Although spoken language is distributed throughout the left hemisphere, the temporal lobe is primarily where language is found within the brain. Wernicke's area, a highly specialized region of the temporal lobe, interprets incoming speech and allows us to understand language. Without Wernicke's area, you could have perfect pronunciation, but words would simply have no meaning.

As we have discussed, the left temporal lobe is a highly specialized area for language; however, it must work synergistically with other regions of the brain to make language complete. For example, corresponding areas of the right temporal lobe are activated during this process to interpret the emotional state of the message to understand voice tones, metaphors, and figures of speech. This is the area of the brain that allows us to "read between the lines." The right temporal lobe also works closely with the parietal lobe (our next stop) to interpret facial expressions and gestures (Carter, 1998).

Parietal Lobes

The parietal lobes are found underneath the skull's parietal bone and directly above the temporal lobes (see Figure 1.6). This region extends to the top of the brain and back to the occipital lobes. The parietal lobe is the area of the brain in which we live; it allows us to experience our surroundings by processing all higher sensory information such as touch, judgment of texture, shapes, and our body's orientation in space.

The parietal lobe is the area of the brain in which we live.

If you were making a purchase at a store and needed to get thirty-five cents from your pocket, the parietal lobes would allow you to distinguish quickly and easily the particular sizes, shapes, and textures of the coins. Although we do not know exactly how the brain processes this information between and among the various neural networks, neuroscientists have discovered that the anterior (front) and posterior (back) areas of the parietal lobe must work together to make this possible.

The front region of the parietal lobes receives sensory information from your body to process sensitivity of touch and pain, it assesses the environmental temperature to keep you from being burned or frost-

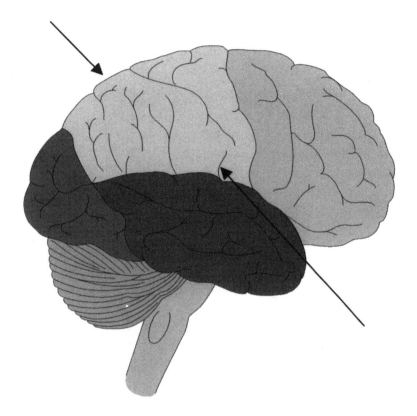

Figure 1.6.   Parietal Lobe

bitten, and it is constantly monitoring your body's orientation in space. There is a specific region in the anterior parietal lobes known as the somatosensory cortex. The purpose of this area of the brain is to process sensory information from the entire body. Each body part has a specific area of representation on the somatosensory cortex. The more important a part of the body is, the greater the area of representation. For example, since the fingers play such an important role in your daily activities, they would have a denser network of neurons in this area than your big toe.

The back area of the parietal lobes integrates sensory information that is essential for analyzing your body's orientation in space as well as the interpretation of spatial relationships. This area of the brain is constantly monitoring and adjusting your body's movements in relationship to your surroundings. The vital sensory information is then sent to the frontal lobes (the final destination of our tour throughout the brain) to allow you to make a conscious and deliberate response to this sensory information.

Frontal Lobes

The frontal lobes are located just under the skull's frontal bone and in front of the temporal and parietal lobes (see Figure 1.7). This area of the brain is what allows you to be who you are. It's where judgment is processed and goal setting is accomplished, where plans are formulated, creativity is constructed, and where your working memory is located. It's the portion of your brain that produces the actual motion of speech in a region called Broca's Area. It's where your ideas and emotions are integrated together to form a conscious thought, and it's the area that creates your unique personality.

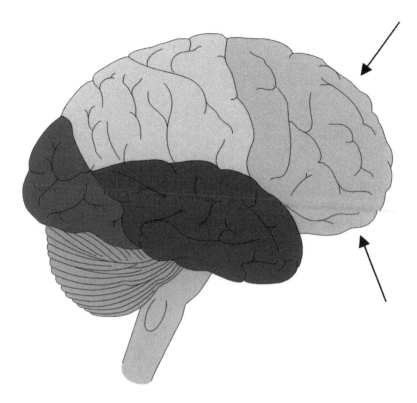

Figure 1.7.   Frontal Lobe

According to research conducted by Richard Davidson at the University of Wisconsin, people who exhibit a more optimistic and positive mood tend to have greater neuronal activity in the left frontal lobe of the brain. Conversely, those who demonstrate a negative and pessimistic attitude reflect more brain activity in the right frontal lobe. In fact, Steve Hyman, Director of the National Institute of Mental Health, stated the way you experience a situation emotionally is reflected by which side of the frontal lobe is more active. If a student perceives a situation as positive the left frontal lobe will be stimulated to produce feelings of optimism. This may explain why some students are eager to attend one teacher's class while being reluctant to enter another instructor's room.

The last area of the frontal lobes that we will discuss is collectively called the prefrontal cortex. This part of the brain is responsible for such characteristics as self-awareness and has the ability to solve complex problems. It is in this area of the brain that you process emotions, sensory information, and cognition into a complete conscious thought. This is also where your working memory is located and is the region in control of making choices and free will. Without the prefrontal cortex, the world would seem meaningless and disjointed, and you would be in a continual state of confusion.

Neurological studies have demonstrated that the prefrontal cortex does not fully develop until the late teens or early twenties. George Bartzokis, a U.S. Department of Veterans Affairs' psychiatrist, reported that this area of the brain may continue to slowly develop until the mid-forties (Bartzokis, 2001). Although this is not a justification for poor behavior, this may be one factor in the inappropriate choices made by some young people.

Deborah Yurgelun-Todd, a neuropsychologist from McLean Hospital in Belmont, Massachusetts, used fMRIs and conducted extensive research to determine if the neural pathways of teenagers were inadequately developed to properly assess fear (Yurgelun-Todd et al., 1999). The teenagers in Yurgelun-Todd's study consistently had difficulty recognizing the expression of fear and showed more activity in the amygdala, the brain's emotional control center, and less stimulation in the regions responsible for decision-making and cognition.

Although teachers cannot accelerate their students' maturation, it is important to design classroom activities that stimulate these regions of the brain. Opportunities to work cooperatively in the classroom, role-playing, debates, participation in character education programs, and other activities that encourage thoughtful reflection about the consequences of right versus wrong may help to compensate for the naturally slow pattern of neuronal maturation.

SUMMARY

We learned that the brain consists of approximately 100 billion neurons and ten times that many glial cells. Learning occurs when there is communication between neurons. Glial cells serve an important supporting function in this process and neurotransmitters play a vital role in how we feel and learn.

Our tour of the brain first took us to the cerebellum, and we learned that it plays a critical role in our ability to move in a smooth and effortless manner. This is also where our "how to" memories are stored as well as the automatic skills associated with reading.

We discovered that the thalamus is referred to as the "gateway" to the cerebral cortex because this is where incoming sensory information is first processed. Our next stop was the hypothalamus, the area of the brain responsible for maintaining homeostatsis, triggering the fight-or-flight response, and working with the pineal gland to regulate our sleeping patterns.

The final stops on our journey were the outermost layers of the cerebral cortex: the occipital, temporal, parietal, and frontal lobes. We learned that each lobe has a specific and vital function: vision is localized in the occipital lobes, language is predominantly found in the temporal lobes, higher sensory information is processed in the parietal lobes, and our ability to formulate a conscious thought is found in the frontal lobes.

In Chapter 2, I will begin the process of applying what you have learned to design a stimulating and intellectually challenging brain-friendly classroom. As you read additional chapters, you may want to refer back to the information contained in this chapter.

Reflect on Chapter 1 for a few minutes to strengthen your neural pathways of learning by making connections (see Figure 1.8).

MAKING CONNECTIONS

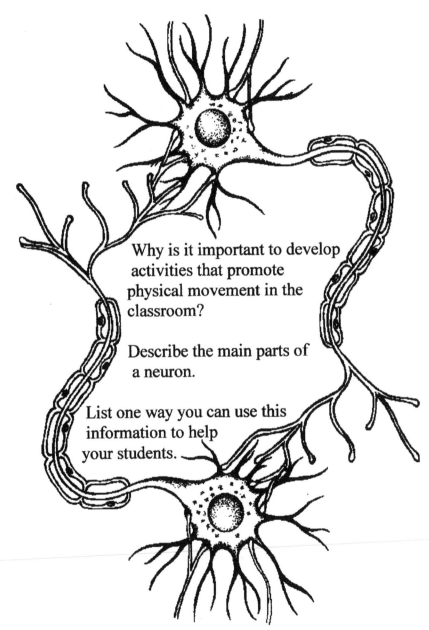

Why is it important to develop activities that promote physical movement in the classroom?

Describe the main parts of a neuron.

List one way you can use this information to help your students.

Figure 1.8.   Making Connections

2

STRATEGIES FOR DESIGNING
BRAIN-FRIENDLY CLASSROOMS

Formal education has become such a complicated and over-regu-
lated activity that learning is widely regarded as something difficult
that the brain would rather not do. Reluctance to learn cannot be at-
tributed to the brain. We are all capable of huge and unsuspected
learning accomplishments.

—Frank Smith, 1986

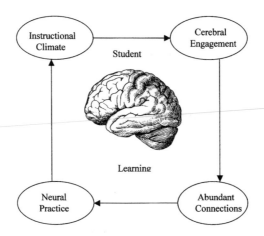

One can rarely read a professional journal or a newspaper, or watch the evening news, without hearing information about recent neurological findings. In view of this research about the human brain, how can educators better help students become more engaged in learning and enhance academic achievement?

There are four steps that teachers can use to integrate brain-friendly learning into the classroom; I refer to this as: *I-CAN*. *I-CAN* is an acronym for *I*nstructional climate, *C*erebral engagement, *A*bundant connections, and *N*eural practice. Meaningful and significant student learning is an interaction between and among these four elements of instruction.

The first step of *I-CAN* is *I*nstructional climate. The design and implementation of a positive instructional climate is one of the most important strategies that teachers can follow to set the stage for brain-friendly learning. The heart of education lies in the ability to establish a cohesive educational team while nurturing meaningful relationships that focus on student learning. Estab-lishing positive professional relationships can help stimulate the production of neurotransmitters and hormones in the brain and body which promote learning and creativity.

> The heart of education lies in the ability to establish a cohesive educational team while nurturing meaningful relationships that focus on student learning.

For a school to be brain-friendly, it should be perceived as a place where individual ideas and thoughts are recognized and valued. To aid in this effort, students and teachers should be able to answer "Yes" to the following three questions:

Three Fundamental Questions

1. *Do I feel accepted and a part of this class and school?*
2. *Do I feel I can make a positive contribution and be successful in this class and school?*
3. *Do I feel physically safe in this class and school?*

These questions address deep underlying psychological needs that are common in all students. One of my favorite quotes is by William James, an early twentieth-century philosopher and educator, who said:

"The deepest principle in human nature is the desire to be appreciated and valued." This is a wonderful statement that is aligned with recent neurological research on the impact that positive emotions and attitudes have on learning (Sapolosky, 1998).

Michele Borba (Bluestein, 1995, p. 3) exemplifies, in the following story, the lasting impact that a teacher can have on students when they feel appreciated and valued.

I'm often asked what influenced me to go into education, and I always say it started with my first grade teacher, Mrs. Fredrickson. From the first day of school at age six, I realized that I never wanted to be anything but just like her, and I've never changed my mind.

Every day when the school bell rang, I knew where I'd find Mrs. Fredrickson. She was always at the door, greeting everyone with what she called "an H or an H," a hug or a handshake. I chose the hug. Most of the kids began with a handshake, but by the end of the first month everybody was going for the hugs.

I remember her being tall, with glasses at the bridge of her nose, but thirty years later, I realize her appearance had nothing to do with the impact she had on me. The impact came from her personal touch, her personal caring, and her ability to make me feel like I was special. Every moment that I was in that woman's room, I felt like I was a "Teacher's Pet."

And now whenever I talk to teachers, I tell them about her. Because when it comes down to how we really and truly can impact kids the most, it isn't the curriculum or some program or kit. We can make such tremendous differences on our students' lives with our personal touch, by greeting them with "an H or an H," and by being a teacher who, like Mrs. Fredrickson, can *really* make them feel special. To me, that's the whole secret to unlocking a child's potential—being there for them, letting them know that we believe in them. What a difference we can make!

If teachers develop such an instructional climate as Mrs. Fredrickson designed in her class, it can produce neurotransmitters in the brain such as serotonin and dopamine that play a crucial part in how students feel and learn. However, when instructors fail to nurture a positive environment, it can create undue stress on the students and have a negative impact on learning, by triggering the production of neurotransmitters and hormones in preparation for the anticipated stressor.

THE IMPACT OF STRESS ON LEARNING

Some stress is inescapable and, in the short-term, modest levels of stress can actually be beneficial. It can enhance your reaction time and make you acutely aware of your physical and sensory surroundings. Moderate levels of stress can aid your memory and serve as a catalyst to help you perform at  your best during challenging situations. However, when modest levels of stress intensify and become routine, your body begins to make radical and profound changes that can have a devastating impact on you. Research studies have consistently revealed that people who endure chronic levels of stress can develop a condition called hypothalamic-pituitary-adrenal cycle that can change the neurochemistry in the body and lead to serious illnesses (see Figure 2.1). This destructive process begins when the body is constantly bombarded with stimuli that produce elevated levels of stress. In preparation for the "fight-or-flight" response, the brain signals the hypothalamus to release a substance called corticotropin-releasing hormone (CRH). The CRH serves as a chemical messenger to alert the body of potential danger. In turn, the CRH signals the pituitary gland to release adrenocorticotropic hormone (ACTH), which triggers the adrenal glands, located on the top of each kidney, to produce large amounts of a steroid hormone called cortisol. When released into the blood stream, cortisol goes throughout the body to mobilize energy reserves, to inhibit the digestive process, and to suppress the immune system. Long-term suppression of the immune system reduces the number of white blood cells in your body and makes you more susceptible to getting sick.

Stress can also have a harmful effect on your vision. Specifically, visual acuity decreases directly in front of your eyes where reading occurs and shifts to the peripheral areas. Although this reaction to stress is usually short-term, students who have existing reading problems may have even more difficulty.

The toxicity produced by excessive levels of the stress hormone cortisol can destroy neurons in an area of the brain called the hippocampus. The hippocampus, referred to as the "gateway to memory," is located in

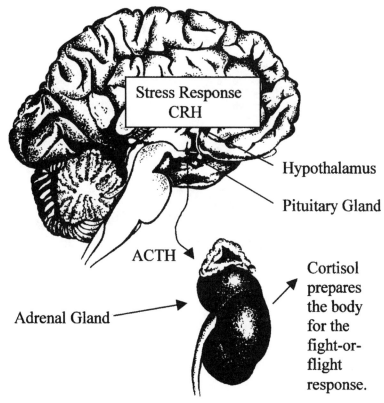

Stress Response
CRH

Hypothalamus

Pituitary Gland

ACTH

Cortisol
prepares
the body
for the
fight-or-
flight
response.

Adrenal Gland

Figure 2.1. Hypothalamic-Pituitary-Adrenal Cycle

the medial temporal lobe and plays an integral role in processing and consolidating all cognitive memories (see Figure 2.2). As information enters the brain from our senses, it is first relayed from the thalamus to the hippocampus where it is compared with previous learning and experiences before being transferred to the working memory. The hippocampus has the unique responsibility of "tagging" facts and information that need to be stored in our long-term memory (Squire & Kandel, 1999). It is almost as if the hippocampus puts a *Post-It* note on important cognitive memories to be stored within the brain.

While sleeping, during the REM sleep cycle, the hippocampus acts like an instant replay to review the experiences you encountered throughout the day (Hobson, 1999). For those experiences that were "tagged" as important, the hippocampus begins the process of transferring this information into various permanent long-term memory

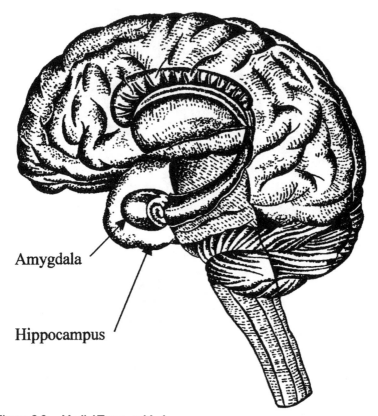

Figure 2.2.   Medial Temporal Lobe

locations in the cerebral cortex. The disturbing news is that neurons of people who constantly experience high levels of intense stress can die due to the toxicity of stress hormones within the brain.

Another result of intense stress is that it limits your ability to think logically and rationally, especially if there are strong emotions attached to the experience.

When there are strong emotions attached to an experience, the amygdala becomes highly active (see Figure 2.2). The amygdala is another brain structure that is buried deep within the temporal lobe. It is highly involved in responding to stress and novel situations, and it mediates all emotionally charged experiences.

The amygdala forms unconscious emotional memories in much the same way as the hippocampus lays down cognitive memories (LeDoux, 1996). As I have previously stated, everything coming in from the senses, with the exception of smell, goes first to the thalamus where it is sorted, catalogued, and sent to the appropriate processing areas in the brain. Emotional information is channeled between two separate pathways before it ends up at the amygdala to create an emotional reaction.

> The amygdala responds to stress and novel situations, and it mediates all emotionally charged experiences.

One pathway in which emotionally laden information can travel increases the heart rate, slows digestion, produces the fight-or-flight response, and alerts the autonomic nervous system to potential danger. This pathway is designed to react quickly in response to incoming information; therefore, there is a network of nerve fibers directly connecting the thalamus to the amygdala. William James said more than a century ago, this system triggers the response to "run away first, and feel afraid later."

The second pathway analyzes the incoming sensory data and compares it to previous memories. This pathway makes the finer discriminations and associations about the nature of the stimulus and determines if there is a reason to be alarmed. The information traveling the second pathway generates a more intellectual and logical response to the stimulus; however, this route takes more time to process before reaching its final destination: the amygdala.

I would like to share a true story that happened to me that illustrates the power of emotions, basically the actions of the amygdala in our lives.

One sunny afternoon, I was traveling home from East Tennessee State University where I had attended a conference on traumatic brain injury. As I was driving down the road reflecting over the speaker's key points, I came upon a stop sign where I came to a complete halt. Well, at least I thought I had come to a complete stop. I proceeded down the road until I heard the distressing sounds of a police siren. Not thinking that I was the intended target, I pulled over to allow the officer to pass. I was shocked when the officer abruptly stopped behind my car.

As the officer approached my car, I noticed he appeared to be very upset. The first words out of his mouth were: "Why did you run that stop sign and why didn't you pull over?" The more he talked, the more he became irate and almost out of control. To make a long story short, I noticed this man did not have any form of identification on his uniform;

therefore, I asked to see his badge. He responded in an angry manner by quickly returning to his car.

Hoping to diffuse the situation and talk my way out of the almost certain ticket, I decided to walk back to his car and talk with him. Before my foot hit the pavement, I heard an earsplitting shout: FREEZE! As I looked up, I was looking down the barrel of his revolver. There I was in a suit and tie, facing a loaded gun, and I was stunned. My amygdala became highly reactive and I just stood there in the middle of the road unable to respond! Finally, I was able to regain my composure, and I patiently waited to accept my ticket!

To this day, if I am driving down the road and see a police officer following me, my blood pressure shoots up, my heart starts beating faster, and I find myself right back in that sunny afternoon on March 16, 1999, looking down the barrel of a loaded gun!

I know that this police officer was an exception, and the majority of officers are highly trained professionals who do an outstanding job. However, having this knowledge is no consolation when I see a police car in the rear view mirror. When this occurs, my amygdala "kicks-in" and I almost hyperventilate!

Students can experience similar reactions in our classrooms. When this occurs, you can forget teaching higher order thinking and creativity because it is not going to happen, especially when students have a history of academic failure and not doing well in school. Maybe something you say triggers previous unpleasant or frightening memories and the student withdraws or overreacts to a situation. If this happens, it is difficult to try to reason with the student in this state. If you need to talk with a student who is in a highly emotional state, it would be helpful first to allow the child to take a brief walk or perform some other repetitive movement before engaging in a discussion. Walking and other repetitive movements have a calming effect by producing dopamine. It's a good strategy to allow a student to stimulate the so-called pleasure center of the brain and allow the amygdala to return to normal. Keeping this in mind can help to prevent inappropriate behaviors from escalating out of control.

> If you need to talk with a student who is in a highly emotional state, it would be helpful to allow the child to take a brief walk or perform some other repetitive movement before engaging in a discussion.

Before I discuss strategies that create a positive classroom climate, let's first take a look at your personal level of stress.

WHAT'S YOUR STRESS LEVEL?

A significant amount of research has revealed that teachers often experience elevated levels of stress during the school day. There are numerous factors that can increase a teacher's level of stress: ambiguity of job expectations, low student motivation, lack of administrative support, unreasonable emphasis on accountability, low wages, high-stakes standardized testing, and the list goes on and on. No wonder it has been said that the stress level of teachers is second only to air traffic controllers (Pam Robbins, personal communication, July 23, 2000)!

According to George Koob (1999) of Scripp Institute, it is not uncommon for people who work in stressful situations to activate the hypothalamic-pituitary-adrenal cycle (see Figure 2.1) as a result of frequent job stress. When this occurs, it can alter your neurochemistry and put your body on a heightened state of alert. This condition can diminish your proficiency for critical thinking and creativity and it impacts your ability to make rational decisions. Therefore, before teachers can effectively design and implement a brain-friendly classroom, they must first manage their own level of stress. With this in mind, let's take a few minutes to complete the *Life-Change Index Scale* (Holmes & Rahe, 1967).

> Before teachers can effectively design and implement a brain-friendly classroom, they must first manage their own level of stress.

Life-Change Index Scale

To learn the level of personal stress in your life, circle the value at the right for each of the following events if it has occurred within the previous 12 months.

Event	Value
Death of spouse	100
Divorce	73

Event	Value
Marital separation	65
Jail term	63
Death of close family member	63
Personal injury or illness	53
Marriage	50
Fired from job	47
Marital reconciliation	45
Retirement	45
Change in family member's health	44
Pregnancy	40
Sexual difficulties	39
Addition to family	39
Business readjustment	39
Change in financial status	38
Death of close friend	37
Career change	36
Change in number of marital arguments	35
Mortgage or loan over $10,000	31
Foreclosure of mortgage or loan	30
Change in work responsibilities	29
Son or daughter leaving home	29
Trouble with in-laws	29
Outstanding personal achievement	28
Spouse begins or ceases working	26
Starting or finishing school	26
Change in living conditions	25
Revision of personal habits	24
Trouble with boss	23
Change in work hours, conditions	20
Change in residence	20
Change in schools	20
Change in recreational habits	19
Change in religious activities	19
Change in social activities	18
Mortgage or loan under $10,000	17
Change in sleeping habits	16
Change in number of family gatherings	15

Event	Value
Change in eating habits	15
Vacation	13
Holiday season	12
Minor violation of the law	11

How to analyze your score: Add the circled values. The higher the score, the harder you need to work at staying physically and emotionally well. If your overall score is above 150, you should consider developing a personal stress management plan. James Messian of Coping.Org. recommends the following steps to reduce stress in your daily life:

- Become familiar with what causes your stress.
- Practice recognizing the stress level when one of these events happens.
- Develop strategies about the different ways you can adjust to the event.
- Practice relaxation techniques: listening to music, meditation, and reflection.
- Maintain a regular and reasonable exercise program.
- Develop a network of support from your family and friends.
- Look for the good in every situation.
- If the stress continues, seek professional help.

CREATING AN OPEN AND POSITIVE INSTRUCTIONAL CLIMATE: SIX BUILDING BLOCKS

An open and positive instructional climate is essential to creating a brain-friendly classroom. Figure 2.3 illustrates the six building blocks teachers can use to make their classrooms more open and positive.

Positive Rapport

Establishing positive rapport with your students is the foundation for creating an open and positive instructional climate. Students need to feel safe and have a sense of cohesiveness and belonging before true learning can occur. This type of learning environment can only be created by

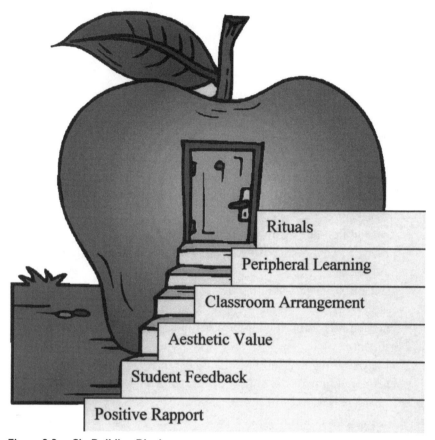

Figure 2.3.   Six Building Blocks

establishing a personal relationship with each student in the class. I have found the following techniques to be effective at all school levels.

Stand at the classroom door and greet each student as often as possible. A powerful technique to establish positive rapport is to offer a warm smile, handshake, or a friendly pat on the back as each student enters the classroom, just as Mrs. Fredrickson did with her first grade class.

> A powerful technique to establish positive rapport is to offer a warm smile, handshake, or a friendly pat on the back

The appropriate use of touch can foster a sense of security and triggers the production of neurotransmitters that are important for learning. One such neurotransmitter is serotonin, which acts as a mood regulator and helps us to be emotionally well-balanced. When students feel stressed or anxious, those feelings can deplete the serotonin levels. Too little serotonin can contribute to having a short attention span and being impulsive, and it can increase aggressive behavior (Carter, 1998).

A second neurotransmitter that may be produced by the appropriate use of touch is dopamine. As I discussed in Chapter 1, dopamine stimulates the pleasure pathways in the brain and almost instantly provides a sense of relaxation and pleasure. When this occurs, it helps to enhance the student's ability to pay attention.

Acknowledge each student by name. A student should hear his or her name called in a positive manner each class period. Nothing is more motivating than hearing your name. This is a powerful strategy to use when designing a brain-friendly instructional climate.

Keep a personal journal for each student. Maintaining a personal journal is an effective strategy to build positive rapport with each student. I asked Marian Diamond (personal communication, January 3, 2000), a renowned neuroscientist from the University of California at Berkeley, what was the most important thing a teacher could do to establish positive rapport with his or her students. She immediately responded: Get to know the students on a personal level; know what's important to each student, what he or she likes or dislikes, and get to know about each student's family. Diamond, who teaches neuroanatomy, keeps a personal journal on each student in her class and uses this information to build positive relationships with her students.

Message signs/posters. As students enter and exit my classroom, they see signs and posters that are located at eye level. The message is simple: Welcome to Class. I am glad you're here. As the students leave a second poster states: Thanks for being in class today. The first and last thing that students see as they enter and leave the classroom are positive statements that convey I am glad they are in class.

Place the teacher desk close to the students. The teacher's desk should be near the students to promote a sense of belonging and security.

Identity posters. Using identity posters is another technique to build rapport with the students by getting to know them on a personal level (see Figure 2.4). Identity posters can be created by dividing a poster board into four sections and having students fill in the details. When the students have completed their identity posters, they can be placed at the back of the classroom on an "Identity Wall."

Student Feedback

Terry Deal, from Vanderbilt University, once said: "Common sense is so uncommon!" Student feedback seems to fall into this category of common sense. Teachers know the importance of this concept; however, the classroom is such a busy place that sometimes we are slow providing feedback.

Establishing meaningful and corrective feedback provides students an opportunity to refine their skills and reinforce what they are learning. It is difficult for students to move forward academically unless they know how they are doing. Each time a student receives feedback, it serves as a catalyst to refire the network of neurons that are responsible for remembering the concept or idea (Squire & Kandel, 1999). Feedback can also make the memories significantly stronger.

> Establishing meaningful and corrective feedback provides students an opportunity to refine their skills and reinforce what they are learning.

Family	Favorite Things to Do/Hobbies
Career Goals	Achievements

Figure 2.4.   Identity Poster

John Hattie (1992), an educational re-
searcher, reviewed over 8000 studies on student achievement and concluded: The most
powerful modification that enhances achievement is feedback. The most effective feedback to enhance memory and improve reten-

> The most powerful
> modification that
> enhances achievement
> is feedback.

tion involves explaining to the students what is correct, what is incorrect
regarding their answers, and allowing them an opportunity to rework the
assignment. According to Robert Marzano, from Mid-continent Research
for Education and Learning (2001), simply telling students if their answers are correct or incorrect can have a negative effect on learning. Students should receive some form of feedback within the classroom approximately every thirty minutes. The feedback can be either teacher or
student directed and should provide a meaningful assessment of the student's progress. Classroom examples of feedback will be provided next.

Stoplight feedback. This technique can be used at the elementary
school level. Students are provided three small three by five inch index
cards each with a picture of a stoplight. One card has the red light com-
pletely shaded, the second has the yellow light darkened, and the third
card has the green light filled-in. To avoid embarrassment, each student
should hold the cards in the palm of his or her hand. As the teacher asks
a question, if the student understands, he or she holds up a green card;
a yellow card would indicate confusion; and the red card means the student does not understand the concept (see Figure 2.5).

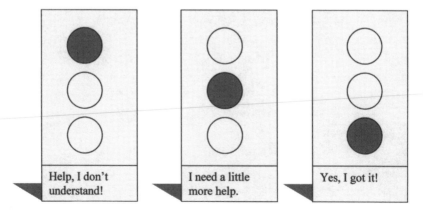

Figure 2.5.   Stoplight Feedback

The following suggestions can be used with all grades by adapting for the students' age.

Brain power teams. Students are organized into groups of two or three and briefly share what they learned in the lesson. This provides a safe environment where students can confirm their knowledge about the subject and assist others in the group who need help.

Critter toss. I purchase "squeaky toys" from the local pet store to use for this activity. Standing at the front of the classroom, I ask a question pertaining to a lesson's objective, wait for approximately four to five seconds, and toss the "critter" to a student. The student answers the question and throws the object back to me. This provides quick feedback to assess the students' knowledge of the subject.

Potpourri of feedback ideas. The following are student-directed feedback techniques: journal writing, peer editing, self-assessment rubrics, self-checking station with random answers, mind-maps, predictions, and share/pairs.

Aesthetic Value

The classroom color and amount of natural lighting influence learning. The brain craves high contrast and novelty and is constantly seeking ways to be stimulated.

The use of color in the classroom is an effective strategy to stimulate the brain and improve memory. Robert Gerard of UCLA conducted research on the physiological effects of color on pulse rate, anxiety, arousal, and blood flow (Jensen, 1995). His conclusion was that every color has a specific wavelength that affects the brain and body differently. Teachers and administrators can use this knowledge in the classroom to impact student learning.

In general, pale yellow, off-white, beige, or pale blue tend to be colors that promote optimal learning and are excellent choices to use in a classroom. Colors that have a tendency to produce a calming tranquil affect are green, purple, or pink with gray as the most neutral color. Bright colors such as red or orange can stimulate creativity and increase a student's energy level. The downside to using bright colors is they can increase aggressive and inappropriate behavior depending on the student's emotional state (Howard, 2000).

Color scheme   Consider painting your classroom one of the colors or a combination of the colors that foster optimal learning: pale yellow, off-white, or pale blue. A shade of pale green, purple, pink, or gray is a good color choice to use in the hallways, cafeteria, and common areas. Avoid using bright red or orange as a room or accent color.

Use color to emphasize key concepts. For information that students absolutely must remember, write the material in green. I refer to this as a "Go Concept"; whenever students see information in green they know it is especially important.

Note-taking and mind-maps. Encourage students to use colored pencils while taking notes or completing mind-maps. The brain remembers color better than the mundane markings from a pencil or pen.

Use color to strengthen learning. Use colored handouts and transparencies to spark learning and memory.

Be consistent. Be consistent once you have selected colors to use in the classroom. Changing colors will confuse students. For example, if green is chosen as the "Go Concept" for important information, always use this color for similar material.

Natural lighting   The amount of natural lighting and full-spectrum lighting influences student achievement, absenteeism, and behavior. A research study conducted by Warren E. Hathaway of Hathaway Planning and Consulting Services studied 327 fourth grade students from the Edmonton, Alberta School District (1995). The results of the two-year study concluded that students who were exposed to full-spectrum lighting with ultraviolet supplements showed greater academic gains, better school attendance, and developed fewer cavities as compared to students under high-pressure sodium vapor lights. Full-spectrum lighting provides the complete color range of natural outdoor light and produces a continuous bright white illumination in the classroom. This lighting is manufactured under brand names such as Vita-Lite and ParaLite. In contrast, most

high-vapor sodium vapor lights generate a flickering light and cast a yel-
lowish or green tint. For additional information, refer to the following
web-sites: *http://www.fullspectrumsolutions.com, http://naturallighting.*
com, and *http://www.designshare.com.*

Research conducted by Pacific Gas and Electric Company (Un-
published, 1999: *http://www.pge.com/pec/daylight/valid.html*) evalu-
ated over 21,000 elementary school students in California, Colorado,
and Washington regarding the impact that natural lighting has on academic performance. The study concluded that students who had the
most exposure to daylight in their classrooms advanced 20 percent
faster in math and 26 percent faster in reading compared to students
with the least amount of natural light.

⬧ *Expose students to daylight.* If your classroom has windows, keep
the shades open and allow daylight to enter your room. If you work in a
windowless classroom, weather permitting, take your students outside
for a few minutes each day to absorb natural light.

⬧ *Supplement your classroom lighting.* Supplement your classroom
lighting by using desk and floor lamps. The additional light in the classroom may decrease the production of cortisol and melatonin levels. A
reduction of cortisol will reduce stress and lowering of the hormone
melatonin will keep students more alert and responsive.

Classroom Arrangement

The configuration of the classroom and the arrangement of student
desks have an impact on learning. Seating arrangements that promote a
sense of cohesiveness are ideal for brain-friendly classrooms. Eric
Jensen (1995) cited research conducted by R. Wlodkowski who recommended classrooms where student desks are arranged in a circle, V-for-
mation, rectangle, or U-formation. This type of classroom organization
helps to establish an atmosphere that allows students to be part of the
group. It is important to periodically rearrange the students' seating assignments. By changing the seating arrangements, students are provided with a new physical perspective for learning, another location for
memory association, and another way to stimulate neuronal growth.

🖝 *Change seating arrangements at the beginning of a new teaching unit.* Changing seating arrangements at the beginning of a new teaching unit or assignment allows students to connect the learning to a new location in the classroom. However, reassigning seating locations too frequently can create undue stress and confusion. The recommended time to change students' seating arrangement is once every three to four weeks or at the beginning of a new and significant instructional unit.

Peripheral Learning

Peripheral learning can be just as effective as traditional instruction. The brain can only focus strongly on one concept at a time; however, it is unconsciously making countless decisions every second. Candace Pert (1997), a neuroscientist from Georgetown University Medical Center, states that 98 to 99 percent of learning is accomplished unconsciously by our brain and body. Research studies have demonstrated the use of peripheral learning (mind-maps, graphic organizers, contextual maps, posters, pictures, music, or written affirmations such as "You can do it.") can make a significant impact on memory.

Colin Rose (1985) cited research by George Lozanov on peripherals in recalling information. A group of 500 high school students was shown a list of ten towns. Five of the towns were slightly underlined in color. The students were given three minutes to memorize the list of towns and showed a much greater recall for the color-coded material. In fact, students were able to remember the underlined material better for a longer period of time. After two weeks, the retention of the consciously learned material declined from 80 to 50 percent; however, the recall of the peripheral information increased from 85 to 91 percent.

🖝 *Pre-expose students to new information.* Prior to teaching a new lesson or unit, expose students to the key information through posters, mind-maps, or graphic organizers. Identify a location in the classroom and use it consistently for this purpose. The material should be placed slightly above eye level. Since the brain can consciously process only one concept at a time, place the peripherals away from the area where you are teaching.

🐛 *Mind-mapping daily lessons.* Students who use mind-maps can consistently recall more information. As a closure activity for each lesson, construct a class mind-map of the main objectives. Use pictures, colors, and contrast to promote better retention. Be sure to keep the mind-map and use it to review the material.

🐛 *Affirmations.* Place affirmations around the classroom for the students. Examples include: "I'm glad you're in class", "Learning is fun!", "Thanks for being in class today!", "Anything is possible", or " You CAN do it." Change the affirmations every three to four weeks.

Rituals

Rituals promote a sense of continuity and security. They help to create a feeling of predictability by establishing a routine for the students. Harry Wong (1998) refers to rituals as developing classroom procedures. He advocates that effective teachers rehearse classroom procedures with their students until they become routine.

The rituals I have developed begin as the students arrive to class. I greet each student at the door with a handshake and a sincere statement. "Hey Conner, I'm glad to see you today"; "Wow Jennifer, I like your new sweater"; or "Hi Stacy, thanks for working so hard in class yesterday." As the students enter the classroom, I have energizing music playing and a colorful overhead transparency that says "I'm glad you're in class!—Please complete your mind-maps." When the tardy bell rings, the students know to immediately complete a mind-map of the previous day's lesson. While the students are working on their mind-maps, I take attendance. For the next ritual, I play two minutes of upbeat music. During this time the students stand up and share what they have written on their mind-maps with a partner. This provides an excellent review of the previous day's lesson. The rituals that I use only take five to six minutes to complete; however, they provide a safe and predictable method to start each class period. For rituals to be effective, they must be performed often and with consistency.

🐛 *Establishing classroom rituals.* The following is a list of additional rituals: start each class with a brain teaser or riddle, play music appropriate for the learning situation, develop procedures for make-up work when students are absent, give students a copy of your weekly lesson plans/activities at the start of each week, complete a reflection journal at the end of each class, establish positive affirmations (such as "Learning is Fun" or "We've got it") and celebrations (for specific celebrations I play the song *Celebrate* by Kool and the Gang), select a "call back song" when students are on break (I play *Back in the Saddle Again*), play a song at the end of the day as students prepare to go home (I play *Na Na . . . Goodbye* by Steam), or give students a high-five as they leave the classroom.

Finally, ask your students to help brainstorm classroom rituals. Just be sure each ritual has a specific purpose, every student knows the procedure, and be as consistent as possible.

SUMMARY

In Chapter 2, you learned how stress impacts learning by triggering the hypothalamic-pituitary-adrenal cycle. Prolonged periods of intense stress can damage the hippocampus, an area of the brain associated with memory. When this occurs, it will be difficult to learn new information. You learned that teaching is a stressful occupation. Before teachers can effectively implement a brain-friendly classroom, they must first manage their own levels of stress.

You discovered the amygdala forms unconscious emotional memories and reacts to stressful and novel situations. Emotional information is processed between two separate pathways: one produces a fast emotionally reactive response while the other generates a slower more logical reaction.

I discussed six strategies that teachers should address when establishing an effective instructional climate. The techniques were positive rapport, student feedback, aesthetic value, classroom arrangement, peripheral learning, and rituals. Specific suggestions were provided for each of the six components of instructional climate.

In Chapter 3, I will discuss how memories are formed and provide ideas to encourage learning and promote the retention of new information. First, however, let's review what you have learned in Chapter 2 (see Figure 2.6).

MAKING CONNECTIONS

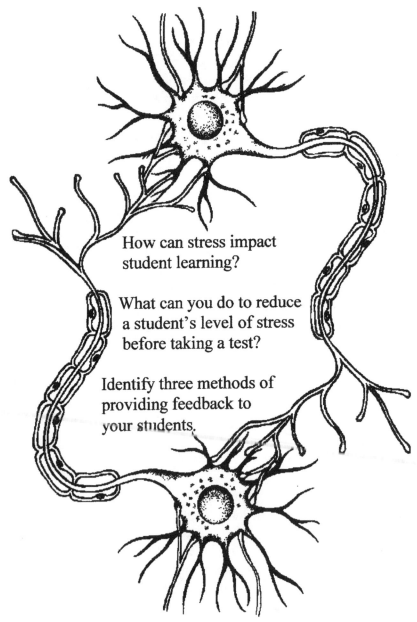

How can stress impact
student learning?

What can you do to reduce
a student's level of stress
before taking a test?

Identify three methods of
providing feedback to
your students.

Figure 2.6.   Making Connections

3

CEREBRAL ENGAGEMENT: THE PATHWAYS TO MEMORY

Without memory, our awareness would be confined to an eternal present and our lives would be virtually devoid of meaning.

—Daniel Schacter, 2000

Learning is the ability to acquire new information or knowledge. Memory is the construction and retention of this knowledge. Without the ability to form and retain new memories, you would be living moment-to-moment. You could not learn from your mistakes or make plans for the future. Life would exist only in the present.

The ability to recall a specific memory is the only evidence that learning has occurred. In essence, you are what you remember. Therefore, teachers are faced with the challenge to understand how memory is processed and how to apply this knowledge in the classroom.

The brain simultaneously processes a multitude of stimuli. It is constantly looking for patterns and associations, and it strives to make sense out of the environment. Our senses are continually collecting and sending information to the brain. Scholars estimate the brain analyzes approximately 40,000 bits of information every second (Sousa, 1995) and makes decisions about this sensory input in a millisecond: one-thousandth of a second!

After you have read this sentence, think about all of the sensory information your brain just processed. The sounds in your room—the hum of the computer or the buzz of fluorescent lights; your clothes—whether they are too tight or too loose; the sounds of an airplane overhead or a police siren in the distance. If you were aware of this constant stimulation, your brain would be on sensory overload and create a condition of *paralysis by analysis*!

GETTING THE BRAIN'S ATTENTION

Candace Pert, author of *Molecules of Emotions*, speculated that 98 to 99 percent of what the brain does is done unconsciously. If information is processed, decisions are made, and new learning is accomplished without your awareness, how can you get the brain's attention? There are three situations that instantly trigger the brain's awareness: survival, emotions, and novelty.

- Survival includes physical survival and attachment survival. The brain is "hard-wired" for physical survival and will immediately focus on anything that is perceived as a threat. If a student is being "bullied" or threatened in class, his or her attention will be focused on the threat and not on the lesson. Attachment survival is concerned with a student's fear of being ostracized or embarrassed. The brain consciously processes one concept at a time. If a student fears being embarrassed, his or her primary attention will be focused on this perceived risk.
- The brain is sensitive to anything that stimulates emotions: positive or negative. Teachers who creatively use emotions in the classroom increase a student's attention and memory.
- The brain is naturally curious and has an affinity for novelty. Anything that is unique or out of the ordinary will increase a student's attention. To emphasize this point I like to say the brain hates **B.O.** B.O. is an acronym for *Boring* and *Ordinary*. To engage a student's attention, teachers should design lessons rich in novelty and avoid boring and ordinary work.

MEMORY CONSOLIDATION

The brain has an intricate method of storing information. It has an elaborate filing system where neurons are organized into millions and millions of vertical mini-columns or files. Each of these vertical columns, which are referred to as *recognition units*, has the responsibility of performing one function (Carter, 1998). There are recognition units in the occipital lobe that are activated when you look at straight lines, while other recognition units become engaged when viewing geometric shapes. Other areas, located in the temporal lobe, are responsible for recalling proper nouns, verbs, or factual information.

Recognition units are used to file new learning into long-term memory. As incoming information is processed throughout the cerebral cortex, it triggers a unique characteristic of memory. New information is remembered by how it is similar to existing knowledge and recalled by how it is different. It is *not* a good practice to teach concepts that are similar during the same lesson because the information can be "filed" together in recognition units with similar characteristics, making the retrieval process difficult.

New information is remembered by how it is similar to existing knowledge and recalled by how it is different.

MEMORY PATHWAYS

Current research has suggested that memory is stored in five pathways: procedural, automatic, episodic, emotional, and semantic. The memory pathways often intersect and experiences may be simultaneously stored in several pathways. In Chapter 4, I will provide examples of how to stimulate each of the five memory pathways.

Procedural Memory

Procedural memory is processed and stored in the cerebellum. This pathway has been referred to as motor or muscle memory. It provides the "how to" reaction to a cognitive stimulation. Once learned, it becomes permanent and is difficult to unlearn. This type of memory involves learning a physical response in reaction to a sensory input. Playing the piano, writing, brushing teeth, and driving a car are examples of procedural memory.

John Ratey, a Harvard professor and author of *A User's Guide to the Brain*, believes the part of the brain that coordinates movement, the cerebellum, is also the area that stimulates thinking. For example, Albert Einstein, who regularly played the violin, generated many new ideas while playing his musical instrument. New research suggests the engagement of the cerebellum stimulates the whole brain by activating the frontal lobes and enhancing creative thinking. Teachers should develop structured movements for students in every lesson to stimulate neural connections of learning.

> Teachers should develop structured movements for students in every lesson.

Procedural memory classroom activities: critter toss for reviewing concepts, group stretching activities, charades, partner walk and review; provide opportunities for students to run errands, allow frequent water breaks, sixty second exercise break; ask a student to lead the class in a one-minute exercise break, and stand up for a classroom cheer.

Automatic Memory

Automatic memory is also stored in the cerebellum. This pathway stimulates non-motor learning and has been referred to as conditioned-response memory (Squire & Kandel, 2000). It is associated with automatic or reflexive responses and can be a helpful instructional strategy to use in the classroom. Information stored in this pathway includes decoding words (the initial phase of reading), multiplication facts, recitation of the alphabet, rhymes, raps, and jingles. It also includes automatic responses such as: *I say hot, you say cold; I say wet, you say dry; I say over, you say under*. Initially this type of learning takes practice; however, once learned it becomes an efficient method to retrieve information.

Automatic memory classroom activities: flashcards, chants, raps, rhymes, music, sequential clapping, rhythm exercises to embedded key learning concepts, and index cards.

Episodic Memory

Episodic memory, processed in the hippocampus, is the ability to remember facts and events that occur within a specific time and place. This memory pathway integrates thoughts, beliefs, and emotions with how they are related to an event. An example of episodic memory is the September 11, 2001 terrorist attacks on America. Take a few minutes to quietly reflect about this incident: Where were you when you heard about the attack? Who were you with and what were you doing? The memories you recall associated with the terrorist attacks are stored in your episodic memory.

Learning is easily consolidated through the episodic pathway. This form of memory is a natural way to learn and has an unlimited storage capacity. It is made stronger by attaching personal emotions and sensory stimulation such as smells, sights, and sounds. Activating episodic pathways helps to stimulate additional recognition units and neural pathways to store memory; more neural pathways mean a greater chance of remembering information. Teaching to episodic memory is an effective instructional strategy to help students recall information.

Episodic memory classroom activities: field trips, guest speakers, teaching accessories (wearing hats, costumes), demonstrations, models, bulletin boards, changing desk arrangements, teach in another room or location, create stories that embed key concepts, make a video or audio tape, peer teaching, journal writing, use of aroma in the classroom, debate, role-playing, color handouts, hands-on experiences, simulations, games, discussions, quiz show reviews, dramas, projects, and authentic problem-solving exercises.

Emotional Memory

Emotional memory begins in the amygdala and significantly influences the retention and recall of information. The brain remembers information and events in which there is an emotional connection. Think back to your earliest childhood memory. For most people, this first memory is associated with something pleasurable or traumatic. The brain remembers these events because when emotions are activated it increases the production of epinephrine and norepinephrine to solidify the memory.

Educational lessons that trigger a student's emotions will enhance attention and make memory stronger. Using this memory pathway is an efficient method of storing information into long-term memory; however, teachers should be careful to maintain an appropriate emotional balance in the classroom. As discussed in Chapter 2, if the emotional component is too strong, it can diminish learning and memory.

> Educational lessons that trigger a student's emotions will enhance attention and make memory stronger.

Emotional memory classroom activities: have celebrations, use music, teach with special passion, occasionally share success stories, use appropriate humor, create learner curiosity, embed content in dramatic story telling, arrange student presentations, put on a puppet show, and practice positive affirmations.

Semantic Memory

Semantic memory is processed in the hippocampus. This memory pathway is sometimes referred to as *factual memory* because it stores information learned from specific facts, lists, and words. In the classroom, students obtain semantic information from books, lectures, and Internet searches. The majority of instructional activities tend to fall into the semantic memory pathway. This type of learning is difficult, because it requires motivation, practice, and repetition of the material in order for students to remember and retrieve the information. Although it may be difficult to remember information in the semantic pathways, teachers can help students develop instructional strategies and memory techniques to consolidate new learning into long-term memory.

Semantic memory classroom activities: acronyms, mnemonic devices, acrostics, peg systems, jingles, rhymes, chants, mind-maps, graphic organizers, journal writing, associations, and linking systems. I will discuss these examples in greater detail in Chapter 4.

THE 3 "M'S" OF ENGAGING MEMORY PATHWAYS

In the previous section, I discussed the five memory pathways. The next step in designing brain-friendly classrooms is using this knowledge to engage the brain for new learning. There are three strategies that teachers can use when introducing a new concept. I refer to this as *The 3 "M's"* of engaging memory pathways: *M*ovement, *M*usic, and *M*ake them laugh!

Movement

Research conducted over the last five years about movement and learning sends a clear message to educators: Movement enriches the brain and promotes thinking. The same regions that control movement, the cerebellum and mid-brain, are inextricably linked to the areas responsible for stimulating cognition (Diamond, 2000). Additional benefits of movement include increased oxygen and blood flow as well as the release of neurotransmitters responsible for attention and memory.

Movement enriches the brain and promotes thinking.

Classroom passivity reduces academic performance and creativity. Prolonged periods of seatwork require sustained attention and will deplete the brain's energy. According to current research, if students remain seated for more than ten minutes it can *begin* to diminish their physical and emotional awareness (Cranz, 1998). Confucius reflected on the negative impact of sedentary learning when he said, "What I hear, I forget, What I see, I remember, What I do, I know." Students need to engage in purposeful physical movement and learn by doing. Any brief break or activity that includes physical movement helps to restore and replenish the brain's energy levels.

Research has consistently confirmed the positive educational outcomes of stimulating the body-mind connection through movement. In a study of over 500 high school students, those who spent an hour each day in physical education class significantly outperformed less active students on exams (Hannaford, 1995). Activities such as aerobic games, running, and jumping have been found to increase students' abilities of mental concentration. According to the Woodcock-Johnson Test of Concentration, students in grades two through four who participated in structured physical activities during the day scored significantly higher on concentration and attention tasks as compared to children who were less active (Caterino & Polak, 1999).

The "Brain Gym," developed by Paul and Gail Dennison (1994), is a beneficial movement program with practical classroom applications. These activities are designed to engage the brain in three areas: laterality (communication between the right and left hemispheres), focus (activation of the frontal lobes and brainstem), and centering (coordination between the cerebral cortex and the emotional center of the brain). Teachers lead students through simple physical exercises that help the brain to integrate and function more efficiently.

Classroom activities: lead students in Brain Gym activities, provide exercise and stretch breaks before tests or activities that require concentration, encourage students to take three deep breaths before each new learning experience, have students demonstrate learning by acting out concepts, use energizers like "Simon Says" or synchronized clapping, celebrations, and water or bathroom breaks; use pantomimes, creative reenactments, a brief walk to reflect over the lesson, educational scavenger hunt, ball or "critter" toss, and recess.

Music

The use of music is an excellent strategy to embed key concepts and prepare students for new learning. Music provides a whole-brain massage to stimulate the neural pathways for attention, increases energy levels, and integrates thinking and creativity. Jeannette Vos, author of *An Introduction to the Music Revolution,* lists eight benefits of using music in the classroom.

> Music provides a whole brain massage to stimulate the neural pathways for attention, increases energy levels, and integrates thinking and creativity.

♪ *Music is a state-changer.* The first step in an effective lesson is to foster a relaxed emotional state for learning. Students who are in unsettled states (tense, angry, or bored) have difficulty assimilating and remembering information. The use of appropriate music is an effective method to change a student's emotional state.

♪ *Music is mathematical.* Certain musical compositions, such as Mozart's Sonata for Two Pianos, stimulate neural pathways associated with decoding complex ideas and solving spatial reasoning problems.

♪ *Music relaxes the brain.* Music can relax the brain by increasing the alpha levels. Alpha level is the brain-wave frequency associated with relaxed alertness and creativity.

♪ *Music inspires emotions.* Music can activate the brain's emotional centers and enhance long-term memory by creating feelings like excitement, courage, or compassion.

♪ *Music stimulates and awakens the learner.* Listening to music can be energizing by increasing the blood and oxygen flow to the brain.

♪ *Music influences the body.* Music can impact metabolism and heartbeat and trigger the release of endorphins, producing a tranquil state of accelerated learning.

♪ *Music is a learning anchor.* The use of dramatic music is a powerful anchor to solidify learning into long-term memory.

♪ *Music is a universal language.* Music has the ability to cross cultural and ethnic barriers. It can set the stage for lessons in any subject area (Vos, 2001).

There are direct relationships between music and academic performance. In 1995 and 1999, the College Board reported a positive correlation between music instruction and performance on Scholastic Aptitude Tests. Students with musical experience scored fifty-one points higher on the verbal portion of the test and thirty-nine points higher on the math section than their non-musical peers. In another study, second grade students at the 95th Street School in the Los Angeles Unified School District participated in keyboard instruction for forty-five minutes each week. After eight months of training, those students increased their average on the national Stanford 9 math scores from 30th percentile to 65th percentile (Shaw, 1999).

Music can be used in the classroom in a variety of ways. For example, Bill Farmer, a media specialist at Bach Elementary School in Ann Arbor, Michigan, used music to teach his fourth and fifth grade students about Abraham Lincoln. He played the song, "Lincoln's Last Train Ride," which describes the days after Lincoln's assassination. The song paints a vivid picture of the funeral train as it passed along its route to Springfield, Illinois (Farmer, 2000). The song provided an emotional "hook" that helped students remember the details of Lincoln's assassination.

I use a variety of music every day: classical, easy-listening, jazz, movie themes, and energizing songs. The musical selections depend on the type of learning environment that I am cultivating. On Monday morning, when children are often tired, I'll play upbeat music to set the tone for the classroom. When students are talkative or very active, I'll use background piano or saxophone music by Kenny G., John Tess, or Danny Wright. This music has a calming effect and has proven to be an excellent tool for managing behavior. Finally, I use music whenever the students are reading a book as a class assignment. For example, when the students read *The Outsiders*, a book about juvenile delinquents, I'll play the song "I Fought the Law and the Law Won" at the beginning of each lesson. This becomes the theme song for the book.

The use of music in the classroom is an effective strategy to engage attention, change emotional states, and accelerate long-term memory. Music is a beneficial brain-friendly instructional strategy; however, there should be a deliberate purpose for using it in the classroom.

Classroom activities: use music as a hook for learning, create new words for existing songs that embed new learning: for example, change the words to "Twinkle, Twinkle Little Star" to include new learning concepts; use music to change the emotional states of students; to energize students use songs like Lynyrd Skynyrd's "Free Bird," Ricky Martin's "Livin' La Vida Loca" or selections from the 1950's Rock-N-Roll music; songs to create a calming effect include Disney movie themes, Space Jam, "I Believe I Can Fly," and "Phantom of the Opera Medley;" use music as a transition from one class or lesson to the next; play a song as a closing ritual for the day: "Happy Trails," "Back in the Saddle Again" or "So Long-Farewell" from the Sound of Music soundtrack; play instrumental background while students are working; use a "call-back" song to return from a break: Rocky I theme song, "Walk Right In" by Rooftop, or the theme song from Raiders of the Lost Ark by John Williams; maintain teacher reference books on the subject of music and learning such as *Tune Your Brain* (1997) by Elizabeth Miles, *Nurturing Your Child with Music* (1999) by John Ortiz, and *Music with the Brain in Mind* (2000) by Eric Jensen.

Make Them Laugh

Humor is an effective strategy to prepare the memory pathways for new learning and to increase students' attention. Laughter involves the whole brain and promotes a balance between the two hemispheres. As a student perceives a joke, the left hemisphere begins processing the words. Simultaneously, the frontal lobe analyzes the emotional components and sends the information to the right hemisphere where it is processed to "get" the punch line of the joke. If the joke is funny, a few milliseconds later, the sensory and motor areas of the brain are engaged to produce laughter (Wooten, 1992).

Humor is an effective strategy to prepare the memory pathways for new learning.

Laughter appears to be genetically "hard-wired" in the brain and is observed in infants as young as five weeks. By three to four everything seems funny; the average preschooler laughs more than 300 times a day. As one grows older, the frequency of laughter significantly decreases. Adults average laughing just fifteen times a day (McAllister, 2001).

The benefits of laughter are numerous. Laughter improves blood circulation, increases skin temperature, lowers blood pressure, increases oxygen levels, improves the immune system, releases endorphins, improves memory, and reduces stress hormones leading to a more relaxed state. This sense of relaxation can remain for up to forty-five minutes. A healthy laugh before taking a test or completing a strenuous academic assignment can have a positive impact on student performance.

According to Ed Dunkelblau, director of the Institute for Emotionally Intelligent Learning, humor in school is more than jokes. It involves the teacher being playful, telling stories and amusing anecdotes, and using exaggeration. For a grammar lesson on "debugging sentences," one elementary teacher used a fly swatter and walked around the class reviewing her students' work in search of "bugs" (Allen, 2001). Making students laugh can be a powerful instructional strategy to reduce student stress, enhance attention, and activate the memory pathways.

Classroom activities: keep a humor file, use funny props to get students' attention, subscribe to internet sites for appropriate daily jokes (*www.cleanlaffs.com, http://www.shagmail.com, http://www. funnymail.com/lists*), create humor bulletin boards, allow sixty second humor breaks where you allow students to share appropriate jokes and funny stories, assign a "funny buddy" to encourage laughter, maintain a library of joke books such as *The Laughing Classroom* (1993) by Diane Loomans and Karen Kolberg, and *The Best of Clean Laffs* (2001).

TESTING YOUR MEMORY

In Chapter 3, I have discussed five pathways of memory and strategies to engage the brain for new learning. Before you proceed to the next chapter, take a few minutes to assess your memory ability. Dayatri Devi, of New York Memory and Healthy Aging Services, developed a simple and effective memory quiz to diagnose potential memory problems. The quiz can be effectively used with high school students through adults. Complete each of the questions listed below.

1. Remember these words: *orange, telephone, lamp*
2. Remember this name and address:
   Mary Smith
   650 Park Street
   Athens, New York
3. Who were the past five U.S. Presidents?
   1.
   2.
   3.
   4.
   5.
4. Who were the last three mayors of your city?
   1.
   2.
   3.

5. What were the names of the last two movies you saw?
   1.
   2.
6. What were the names of the last two restaurants in which you ate?
   1.
   2.
7. Have you had more difficulty recalling events from the previous few weeks?
   Yes____ No____
8. Have you noticed a decline in your ability to remember lists, such as shopping lists?
   Yes____ No____
9. Have you noticed a decline in your ability to perform mental math, like calculating change?
   Yes____ No____
10. Have you been more forgetful paying bills?
    Yes____ No____
11. Have you had more trouble remembering peoples' names?
    Yes____ No____
12. Have you had more trouble recognizing faces?
    Yes____ No____
13. Do you find it harder to find the right words you want to use?
    Yes____ No____
14. Have you been having more trouble remembering how to perform simple physical tasks such as operating the microwave or remote control?
    Yes____ No____
15. Does your memory interfere with your ability to function:
    At work?   Yes____ No____
    At home?   Yes____ No____
    In social
    situations   Yes____ No____
16. Without looking, do you recall the three words from the first question?
    1.
    2.
    3.

17. Without looking, do you recall the name and address you were
    given?

1.

2.

3.

Scoring
Questions 3-6: 1 point for each correct answer (12 points)
Questions 7-15: 1 point for each "no" answer (11 points)
Questions 16-17: 1 point for each correct answer (9 points)

Interpretation
28-32 points: You have a better than average memory.
22-27 points: You may need to monitor your memory
                 closely.
0-21 points: You probably need to seek a professional
                 evaluation.

SUMMARY

In Chapter 3, you read that memory is the construction and retention of
knowledge. The ability to recall a specific fact is the only evidence that
learning has occurred.

You learned there are five memory pathways: procedural, automatic,
episodic, emotional, and semantic. As memories are filed in the brain,
the pathways often intersect and experiences are simultaneously stored
in several pathways. You discovered specific instructional strategies to
stimulate each of the five memory pathways.

Chapter 3 concluded by identifying the 3 "M's" of engaging memory
pathways for new learning. The methods were movement, music, and
make them laugh. Movement enriches the brain and promotes thinking,
music stimulates the neural pathways for attention and influences the
emotional states of the learner, and humor reduces stress and increases
oxygen and blood flow.

In Chapter 4, I will provide instructional strategies to engage the five
memory pathways. But first, let's stimulate your dendrites by reviewing
what you read in Chapter 3 (see Figure 3.1).

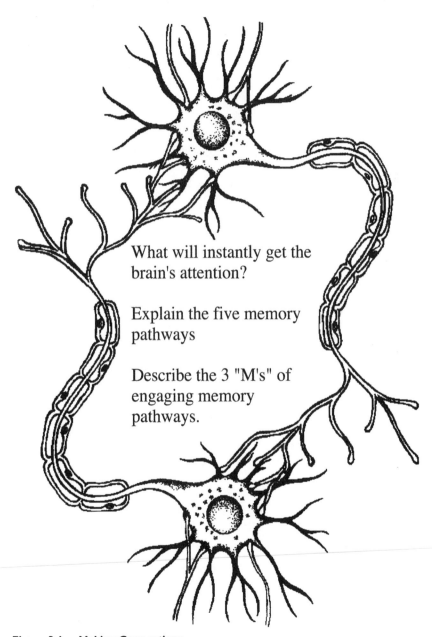

What will instantly get the brain's attention?

Explain the five memory pathways

Describe the 3 "M's" of engaging memory pathways.

Figure 3.1. Making Connections

4

ABUNDANT CONNECTIONS

If someone learning something new is exposed to it only once, whether or not the information sticks will depend upon many factors. These include whether the information is important, whether it is associated with something already familiar, and whether or not the person is paying attention.

—McKhann and Albert, 2002

The third component of the I-CAN Model is developing instructional strategies to help students make *abundant connections*. Learning, from a neurological and physiological perspective, is when dendrites branch out and form new neural connections. Each time these connections are stimulated the memory becomes stronger and easier to retrieve.

Think back to your college days for a simple analogy of this concept. Although most college campuses have an ample supply of sidewalks it seems to be human nature for people to take shortcuts through the grass. The first few times this occurs, there is minimal evidence that anyone has taken this new pathway. However, when students continue to walk over the same area the grass rapidly wears down and forms a noticeable pathway. Learning is similar to this analogy: each time an idea or concept is practiced the neural pathways of learning are stimulated and the memory becomes stronger. Students recall lessons more easily if they have been exposed to similar ideas; what they remember from the past has much to do with what they can learn in the future. When teachers allow students the opportunity to practice, construct, manipulate, and personalize new knowledge with previous learning, they are paving the pathway for a unique phenomenon known as long-term potentiation, or LTP.

LONG-TERM POTENTIATION/THE DOMINO EFFECT

Remember as a child when you meticulously set-up one domino after another and with a gleeful touch of your finger they came cascading down? The childhood game of dominos provides an analogy for the concept of long-term potentiation. Each new experience or learning activity triggers a group of

> Each new experience or learning activity triggers a group of neurons, like dominos, to react in synchrony.

neurons, like dominos, to react in synchrony. When this occurs, a chemical change takes place within the brain that leaves the neurons on a heightened sense of alert and makes it easier to recall the learning experience. If the experience is repeated or reinforced, it causes the brain to produce important proteins that store the event in memory. On the other hand, if students are not provided opportunities to practice a new concept over time the bonds between the neurons will diminish and the memory will fade. Practice really does help make learning permanent.

TYPES OF MEMORY

Memory can be classified into three categories: sensory, active, and long-term and is based on the length of time that the memory exists (Mesulam, 2000). The shortest memory lasting only milliseconds is called sensory memory. The purpose of this memory is to rapidly process incoming sensory information and assess its importance to your survival. The brain maintains the sensory input just long enough to make a decision about it. For example, you notice whether your clothes are too tight or too loose or sounds that are around you. Sensory memory allows your eyes to process individual snapshots of your surroundings as a fluid picture.

Active memory, sometimes referred to as working memory, is a function of the prefrontal lobes and only holds a small amount of information for a short period of time. This type of memory allows you to remember an e-mail address just long enough to type it or to recall a word that you are looking up in the dictionary. Information in active memory is vulnerable to being lost unless it is consciously practiced. Typically, active memory is measured according to the amount of information that can be temporarily remembered and is based on an individual's age. For example, an average eight year old can hold approximately five bits or chunks of information in active memory, while an adult can hold seven bits of information, plus or minus two items.

Long-term memories are stored throughout the cerebral cortex and involve actual structural changes to the neurons. When new information is transferred from short-term to long-term memory there is an increased number of synapses, or connections, between the brain cells (Drubach, 2000). This increase of connectivity enhances the communication between neurons and aids in the retrieval of memories. There can be an unlimited amount of information stored in long-term memory, and it does not require continual rehearsal to be remembered. For instance, factual information such as the capital of Texas is Austin, multiplication facts, or the make and model of your first car are all stored in your long-term memory.

PRIMACY-REGENCY EFFECT

There are many factors that impact a student's retention of new knowledge during an instructional period. One such variable is when a new learning objective is presented during the lesson. To demonstrate this concept, please refer to the list of states. Using a timer or the second hand of your watch, study the states for fifteen seconds. Next, cover the page and write the states in the correct order.

New Hampshire
Massachusetts
New York
New Jersey
Connecticut
Rhode Island
Delaware
Pennsylvania
Maryland
Virginia
North Carolina
South Carolina
Georgia

Unless you are a history teacher and recognized the above states as the original thirteen colonies or used a mnemonic memory strategy, you probably remembered some of the states at the beginning and end of the list but had difficulty recalling the ones in the middle. This is a simple example of the primacy-regency effect: students remember more at the beginning and end of a lesson while having difficulty retaining material in the middle.

> Students remember more at the beginning and end of a lesson while having difficulty retaining material in the middle.

The same concept can be applied to instructional time within the classroom. Students have a limited amount of information that they can absorb before the brain goes on information overload. On average, a student can pay attention and focus on a lesson for approximately two minutes longer than the child's age. For example, if a student is ten years old, he can pay attention for *about* twelve minutes before he starts to lose focus. Using the above example, once a teacher has the learners' attention, information should be presented immediately at the beginning of the lesson, followed with a brief break at the end of twelve minutes to allow students time to process the new learning. During the processing time, for instance, students could complete reflective journal writings, review the material in pair/shares, complete mind-maps, or engage in a class discussion. Planning for the primacy-regency effect will provide more opportunities for students to practice and rehearse new learning, resulting in greater academic achievement.

STIMULATING MEMORY PATHWAYS WITH MNEMONIC STRATEGIES

New knowledge is expanding at an exponential rate and students are required to remember more information than ever before. In addition, high-stakes testing for students and increased standards of accountability are being enforced in almost every state. How can teachers help students retain this vital information while keeping school an energizing and exciting place to be? One brain-friendly method is to teach students to use specific mnemonic strategies to stimulate the neural pathways of learning.

Mnemonic strategies are an instructional method for improving initial learning and promoting long-term retention of important information. The brain is constantly seeking to make patterns and associations with new incoming information and mnemonics are a natural and fun way to tap into this learning opportunity. These strategies help students to remember information more easily by associating new knowledge with something interesting, vivid, or out of the ordinary while stimulating the memory pathways through the use of visual pictures, rhymes, songs, colors, rhythms, or movements.

According to Mastropieri and Scruggs (1991), students who were taught using mnemonics significantly outperformed those who received traditional classroom instruction. Mnemonic instruction is an effective learning strategy applicable to all academic areas. Whenever there is specific content to be recalled, mnemonic strategies are a fun and engaging method to improve memory.

Although there are numerous mnemonic strategies that have been developed, I will discuss five techniques that I have found to be especially useful in the classroom: keywords, pegwords, acronyms/acrostics, body list, and loci technique. These strategies can

> Whenever there is specific content to be recalled, mnemonic strategies are a fun and engaging method to improve memory.

be adapted for all grade levels; however, it is important to remember the amount of information that students can retain in their active memory.

Keyword Mnemonics

The use of keyword mnemonics combines a specific word with the definition of a new word that is easily visualized. To use this idea in the classroom, it is important to develop a picture of the keyword and its definition interacting vividly together. Research demonstrates this to be an effective technique to learn new vocabulary words and a foreign language. The old adage: *A picture is worth a thousand words,* is certainly fitting for this method of instruction.

An example of applying keyword mnemonics is teaching the definition for a new vocabulary word: barrister. A barrister is a British counselor who is allowed to appeal his case to a higher court; therefore, lawyer is a synonym for this word. An appropriate keyword for barrister is bear. Students could create a picture of a big grizzly bear wearing round wire-framed glasses, acting in the courtroom as a lawyer, who is pleading his client's case (Mastropieri & Scruggs, 1998). This silly picture will help students to associate the courtroom "lawyer" bear with the word barrister!

This same strategy can be used to learn a foreign language. Students simply produce a keyword, a corresponding picture, and associate it with the new foreign vocabulary word. An example of this concept is provided below for student learning (Mastropieri & Scruggs, 1991, p.24).

Latin Word and Meaning	Keyword	Corresponding Picture
Mela (apple)	mail	an apple in a mailbox
Lago (lake)	log	a log floating in a lake
Carta (letter)	cart	a cart containing a letter

Pegword Mnemonics

The pegword method links numbers to specific mental images that associate or rhyme with each number. I share the following pegword system with my students to introduce this concept:

one is *sun*   six is *licks*
two is *shoe*   seven is *heaven*

three is (willow) *tree*   eight is (ice) *skate*
four is *floor*   nine is *lion*
five is *hive*   ten is (safety) *pin*

After students have an understanding of this concept, they should be encouraged to create their own list of pegwords. This helps to personalize the learning and allows it to be meaningful for each student. It is easier to use words that can be visualized, and the image should be created in as much detail and animation as possible. For example, if three is tree, what kind of tree is it? Does it have leaves on its branches and what is its shape? The memory retrieval process will be effortless if students give more attention to establishing each image in vivid and colorful detail.

Learners can use pegwords anytime they have to memorize a list or recall specific information in the correct order. For example, if students need to identify the first ten Presidents of the United States, they could associate each President with a pegword. For instance:

Number	Pegword	President	Visual Image Created
1	sun	Washington	The sun's rays are shining so brightly into Washington's eyes, he falls off his white horse.
2	shoe	Adams	John Adams is sitting in his office putting on a pair of red high heel shoes.
3	tree	Jefferson	Jefferson is swinging from the branches of a willow tree with the Declaration of Independence under his arm.

The remaining presidents can be listed using pegword mnemonics similar to these examples. Students love using this memory strategy in class. It is important to create action pictures that are vivid, colorful, and funny.

Acronym and Acrostic Mnemonics

Acronyms and acrostics are two effective mnemonic strategies that use letters or short phrases to help the learner remember vital information.

Acronyms are words that are created by using the first letter of important words to stimulate your memory. For example, "NASA" for the National Aeronautics and Space Administration, "MADD" for Mothers Against Drunk Drivers", and "SAD" for Seasonal Affective Disorder. Several common classroom examples are: "HOMES" for each of the Great Lakes: Huron, Ontario, Michigan, Erie, and Superior; "RACE" for Related Arts Create Excitement; and "LIP" for Lever, Inclined Plane, and Pulley to help children remember three simple machines in physical science.

Acrostics use the first letter of key learning concepts to form a sentence or phrase. The more humorous and witty the sentence, the easier it will be to remember new information. The following are some common and useful classroom acrostics:

Acrostic Mnemonic	Learning Concept
Never Eat Shiny Weeds	For the geographic directions going clockwise: north, east, south, west
I Ate A Pizza	For the four Oceans: Indian, Arctic, Atlantic, Pacific
Eat An Apple As A Nightly Snack	For the seven continents: Europe, Australia, Asia, Antarctica, Africa, North America, South America

The brain hates B.O.: boring and ordinary work! The creative use of acronyms and acrostics can help children retain key learning concepts while creating a fun and engaging learning environment.

The brain hates B.O. boring and ordinary work!

Body List Mnemonics

The body list is one of my favorite mnemonic strategies that I use to help students recall a list of information. I select ten body locations to connect or hook the new learning material. The specific body parts that I use are as follows: head, shoulders, chest, belly button, love-handles, rear, thighs, knees, shins, and toes. Next, as new knowledge is being introduced, I make a funny story to create a vivid colorful image and connect the material to each body part. A high school physical science teacher used this idea to help students classify elements that were nonmetals: hydrogen, carbon, nitrogen, phosphorus, oxygen, sulfur, and selenium. The following is an example for hydrogen: Since hydrogen is the first non-metal, it is connected to the first position on the body list (head) by using this silly story. A student walking down the hallway saw his long-lost friend, Gin. In amazement, he touches his head (the first location on the body list) and shouts: "Hi—Gin" which sounds like hydrogen! Thus, the first non-metal is associated with the first location on the body list. This type of experience gets students actively engaged in the learning process; they laugh, have fun, and most importantly, remember what is being taught.

Loci Mnemonic Technique

The loci mnemonic technique was used by Roman orators over 2,500 years ago to remember their speeches. The word *loci* is derived from the Latin word for place. Therefore, to use this technique, you need to recall a familiar place such as your home in order to store new information in your memory. For instance, select a room in your house such as your kitchen and choose five different locations to attach information you need to remember: microwave, stove, table, refrigerator, and sink. As with the other mnemonic strategies, it is important to create vivid colorful images that are action-packed and animated to associate with each loci position.

A classroom example for using this method can be used to learn early American history. For example, students can use this strategy to remember the five committee members—Benjamin Franklin, John Adams, Roger Sherman, Robert Livingston, and Thomas Jefferson—appointed by Congress on July 2, 1776 to prepare our country's proclamation of independence. The first loci location is microwave; students can create an action-packed image placing a quart of Ben & Jerry's chocolate ice cream (the key word for Benjamin) filled with hotdogs (the key word for Franklin) into the microwave and visualize the results! This humorous picture will connect Benjamin Franklin to the first loci place.

When you need to recall the information, all you have to do is to take a "mental walk" through your kitchen and visualize the items that you want to remember. As you and your students become more proficient using this memory strategy, you can add additional rooms to retain greater amounts of information.

Mnemonic strategies are an effective method to help students remember large amounts of factual information. Teaching students to use these memory strategies will equip them with the necessary tools to be life-long learners. There are numerous teacher-friendly books and websites that provide useful examples of these techniques. The following are some that I have found to be most useful: *Teaching Students Ways to Remember: Strategies for Learning Mnemonically* by Margo Mastropieri & Thomas Scruggs; *Accelerated Learning* by Colin Rose; *How to Develop a Super Power Memory* by Harry Lorayne; Mind-Tools—*http://www.mindtools.com/memory.html*, Brain Connection—*http://www.brainconnection.com/*, and Memory—*http://www.exploratorium. org/memory/index.html*.

CONSOLIDATING TIME: THE GLUE THAT HOLDS LEARNING TOGETHER

Learning, as well as the ability to retain and retrieve memory, takes time and practice. The hippocampus, which is responsible for the storage of new semantic memory, has a limited capacity to hold information. If too much material is presented at one time, the brain will be unable to absorb the data and the knowledge will be lost. Neuroscientists have learned when the brain stores information in long-term memory the neurons undergo a chemical and structural change (Squire & Kandel, 2000). In addition, when the new learning is practiced and rehearsed over time, the neural connections become stronger, and the memory is solidified making the retrieval process easier.

In the classroom, it is counterproductive to try to maintain a student's attention for an extended period because the brain needs time to process new information. As I discussed, as a basic rule, a student can pay attention and focus on a lesson for approximately two minutes more than the child's age. If a student is fifteen years old, he can generally pay atten-

> It is counterproductive to maintain a student's attention for an extended period because the brain needs time to process new information.

tion for approximately seventeen minutes before the hippocampus becomes saturated with information. There are many factors that influence a student's attention and the brain's ability to consolidate new memories. Therefore, I use this formula only as a guide to plan my lessons and activities.

A brief downtime during which the brain does not have to process new information serves as a memory catalyst. For example, it appears that the synapses, the area that dendrites connect to axons, are actually strengthened. In addition, essential proteins are produced which are necessary for the consolidation of long-term memory.

This does not mean that students should be provided new lessons every ten or fifteen minutes; however, it is helpful to stop and allow children time to process the new learning. During this downtime, students can practice the information more in depth by completing reflective journals, practicing reciprocal teaching with a learning partner, taking a "learning walk" with another student to review the lesson, using the activity Pathways of Synergistic Learning, or writing a rap song with the lesson's key concepts. It is essential to schedule time during each lesson for students to refocus, and more importantly, for the brain to encode and begin the consolidation process.

SUMMARY

In this chapter, you discovered the third component of the I-CAN Model is *Abundant Connections*. You learned there are three types of memory: sensory, active, and long-term, and how each new learning experience influences long-term potentiation.

The concept of Primacy-Regency Effect was discussed, and you discovered that learners tend to remember more information at the beginning and end of a lesson; however, they have difficulty retaining material in the middle. In addition, I discussed as a general rule, a student can pay attention for approximately two minutes longer than his chronological age.

You read how to help students make abundant neural connections by using five specific mnemonic strategies: keywords, pegwords, acronyms/acrostics, body list, and loci. In developing these strategies, it is important to create vivid, colorful, humorous, and animated mental images to associate with the new learning.

Finally, in Chapter 4, you read about the importance of scheduling time within the lesson for students to consolidate and process new learning. This will significantly increase the students' ability to retain and retrieve new knowledge.

In Chapter 5, I will discuss methods for students to practice and rehearse new learning. For now, let's review what you learned in Chapter 4 by Making Connections (see Figure 4.1).

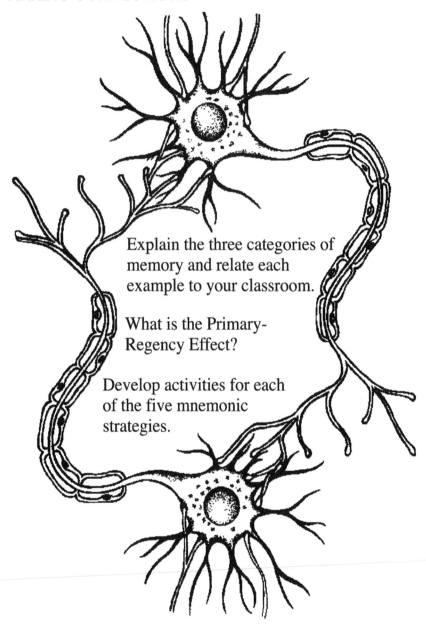

Explain the three categories of memory and relate each example to your classroom.

What is the Primary-Regency Effect?

Develop activities for each of the five mnemonic strategies.

Figure 4.1.   Making Connections

5

NEURAL PRACTICE

> The art of remembering is the art of thinking. When we wish to fix a new thing in either our own mind or a pupil's, our conscious effort should be not so much to impress and retain it as to connect it with something else already there.
>
> —William James

Neural practice is the final step to complete the framework of the I-CAN Model. As William James stated almost 100 years ago, if learners are to remember new information it must be connected with existing knowledge. It is essential that students have the opportunity to practice and rehearse new learning, to personalize and connect it with previous knowledge, and to validate and apply the material through authentic experiences. Providing these learning opportunities is a critical and time-consuming aspect to help students move beyond superficial learning to demonstrate comprehension and in-depth understanding. Learning a new subject matter takes times and requires multiple practice and review sessions.

According to comprehensive research studies in cognitive psychology reviewed by Marzano, Pickering & Pollock (2001), students need to practice and review new content information at least twenty-four times to obtain 80 percent competency. This extended practice period is significant because the brain needs time to consolidate and store new memories. Although twenty-four practice sessions may sound like a high number, it can include homework assignments, daily review, and mind-map activities. Extensive research conducted by J. Allan Hobson (1999), Professor of Psychiatry at Harvard Medical School, has highlighted the importance of REM (rapid eye movement) sleep in long-term memory consolidation. During REM sleep the hippocampus "replays" and rehearses new learning and memory patterns. This process occurs while dreaming and helps to transfer and solidify new experiences into long-term memory. Therefore, providing practice and review activities that are separated by a night of REM sleep are critical components of learning and memory storage.

> Students need to practice and review new content information at least twenty-four times to obtain 80 percent competency.

> Practice and review activities that are separated by a night of REM sleep are critical components of learning and memory storage.

STRATEGIES TO PROMOTE PRACTICE AND REHEARSAL

There are two basic strategies to practice and rehearse new content information: Verbatim Rehearsal and Authentic Rehearsal. However, before students begin to practice new learning, it is essential the information makes sense and the learners understand the material (Sousa, 1995). Higher intellectual thinking skills are diminished if the new knowledge does not make sense and is not personally relevant to the learner.

VERBATIM REHEARSAL

Verbatim rehearsal is when the learner needs to remember subject matter precisely as it was entered into active memory. This includes recalling such information as scientific and mathematical formulas, or semantic knowledge like dates, states and capitals, or the Presidents of the

United States. In other words, students are required to restate, verbatim, content matter back to the teacher. This type of information is difficult for students to remember and traditional schools spend a significant amount of time teaching and testing in this category.

We are teaching a "play-station" generation of students who are comfortable with technology and accustomed to being stimulated by fast-paced sounds and images that are highly animated and visual. As a result, children often become bored when they are expected to sit in class and memorize large amounts of material. In recognizing this fact, teachers may consider designing brain-friendly instructional techniques to help students remember new knowledge. Mnemonic strategies such as I discussed in Chapter 4 are appropriate to use for verbatim rehearsal.

Examples of Verbatim Rehearsal

Students who are required to memorize the states and capitals of the United States can create an action-packed visual image and connect each state with its capital. The following are examples of this method:

State	Capital	Visual Image
Delaware	Dover	A skinny man wearing pink pants is walking into a "deli" (for Delaware) and a "Doberman pinscher" (for Dover) runs up and bites him on his bottom.
Massachusetts	Boston	An employee watches her "boss" who weighs a "ton" (for Boston) walk down the street to attend "Mass" (for Massachusetts).
Kentucky	Frankfort	A man with a gigantic mustache is eating "hotdogs" (for Frankfort) out of an old, rusty can (for Kentucky).

Memorize in Minutes: The Times Tables (Walker, 2000) is a clever program that uses colorful pictures and stories to help students learn and practice the multiplication tables. It integrates visualization, movement, and humor into easy to use and effective learning strategies. This program can be viewed online at: *www.multiplication.com.*

The *Shurley Method* is a brain-friendly instructional program for teaching English grammar and writing. It incorporates rhythmic movements, chants, and jingles into a fun and energizing curriculum where students quickly encounter academic success. The *Shurley Method* includes systematic repetition of key grammatical concepts that help learners retain information quickly and easily. An example is provided below (*http://www.shurley.com/docs/hs_ele.html*).

Noun Jingle
This little noun
Floating around
Names a person, place or thing.
With a knick, knack, paddy wack,
These are English rules.
Isn't language fun and cool?

A final example of verbatim rehearsal during which I help students recall specific semantic information comes from teaching *Romeo and Juliet*. High school English students frequently have difficulty remembering the setting of this play: Verona, Italy. To help overcome this learning obstacle, I ask the students to imagine and vividly visualize they are placing a large cowboy boot on their left foot. The cowboy boot represents Italy, and the top of the boot corresponds to the location of Verona. This silly activity helps to store semantic information into multiple memory pathways and increases the chance students will remember this material.

Providing specific strategies to recall information normally retrieved by verbatim rehearsal will increase the students' level of comprehension and improve academic achievement. However, the ultimate goal is for students to have the ability to transfer and apply this knowledge across the curriculum, and more importantly, to authentic real-life situations.

AUTHENTIC REHEARSAL

Authentic rehearsal is used when it is not essential to remember information specifically as it was entered into memory. This type of rehearsal is complex and promotes intellectual thinking and problem-solving skills. Authentic rehearsal moves the learner beyond mere memorization by encouraging the student to analyze, synthesize, and evaluate knowledge through novel and challenging learning activities. As a result of using this rehearsal strategy, students develop a deeper understanding and demonstrate greater retention of the subject matter.

> Authentic rehearsal moves the learner beyond mere memorization by encouraging the student to analyze, synthesize, and evaluate knowledge through novel and challenging activities.

Examples of Authentic Rehearsal

Activities that use authentic rehearsal stimulate the neural pathways of episodic memory and promote better recall by engaging students in hands-on, authentic, or simulated experiences. For example, a high school English teacher has her class read *Homecoming*, by Cynthia Voigt. This book is written about four children who travel alone from Cape Cod to Maryland's eastern shore. The teacher transformed her classroom into a massive map and students moved around the room to read and complete hands-on activities that correspond to the events in the story.

When teaching about challenges faced by the Pilgrims on the Mayflower, an elementary teacher asked his students to conduct research about the ship's dimensions and living conditions. The students used masking tape to outline the length and width of the Mayflower (ninety by twenty-four feet) on the gymnasium floor. To simulate the crowded conditions for the Mayflower's 102 passengers and 15 crew members, the actual number of students stood within the parameters of the tape while the teacher engaged the children in a stimulating lesson about this historical event.

The results of research studies have consistently demonstrated that a student's level of retention is significantly greater if he is engaged and actively participating in a lesson. Activities such as pair/shares or peer teaching are excellent strategies for authentic rehearsal. When students are responsible for sharing knowledge with others, they are likely to be more attentive to the material. If learners construct their own meaning and articulate this knowledge to others, it will enhance their level of retention and recall.

Additional examples of authentic rehearsal are listed below. These activities can be modified and are applicable for all grade levels.

- Debates
- Reflective journal writing
- Guest speakers
- Historical reenactments
- Students teaching students
- Community service project
- Analogies

- Role-playing
- Field trips
- Student-run store
- Creative controversy
- Learner-led interview
- Student-written newsletter
- Mock trials

- Storytelling
- Recycle program
- Job shadowing
- Review Jeopardy
- Documentaries
- Simulations
- Create models

These activities promote multiple memory pathways, stronger neural networks for new information to be stored in the brain, and are often packed with emotions. When teachers develop meaningful lessons and allow students to practice the learning through authentic rehearsal activities, it stimulates chemicals within the brain which act as a holistic superglue to solidify the knowledge into long-term memory. Students will not only remember the information at test time, but will be able to apply the knowledge to real-life situations.

> When teachers develop meaningful lessons and allow students to practice the learning through authentic rehearsal activities, it stimulates chemicals within the brain which act as a holistic superglue to solidify the knowledge into long-term memory.

A LOOK BACK AT THE I-CAN MODEL

The I-CAN Model provides teachers with a conceptual framework to apply brain research to the classroom. The purpose of this model is to provide teachers with a method to integrate the concepts of brain-

friendly learning into the classroom by being aware of four key elements: Instructional climate, Cerebral engagement, Abundant connections, and Neural practice. It is predicated on the belief that the way to
enhance students' academic achievement is to focus on building positive
relations, on providing a meaningful and challenging curriculum aligned
with the way the brain naturally learns, and, in keeping with the orange-
peel analogy that I shared in the introduction, on the importance of attending to details and doing the little things well.

SUMMARY

In Chapter 5, I discussed the final step of the I-CAN Model: Neural
practice. If students are to retain and retrieve knowledge, they must be
given multiple opportunities to practice and rehearse the new learning.

You learned there are two strategies for students to practice new
learning: verbatim rehearsal and authentic rehearsal. Verbatim rehearsal is when the learner needs to recall the information exactly as it
was entered into active memory. It includes memorizing formulas,
equations, and semantic information like listing the four stages of cell
division or the year that the Declaration of Independence was signed. It
is often difficult for learners to remember this type of information. Students should be encouraged to develop mnemonic memory strategies to
remember information in this category.

Authentic rehearsal is more complex and stimulates intellectual
thinking and problem-solving skills. It moves the student beyond memorization resulting in a deeper understanding of the subject matter. If
students are not allowed to practice and rehearse new learning, it is
doubtful they will retain the knowledge in long-term memory.

In the next chapter, I will discuss ways to keep your brain active and
in top mental condition, but first, let's reflect over Chapter 5 and stimulate your neurons by Making Connections (see Figure 5.1).

MAKING CONNECTIONS

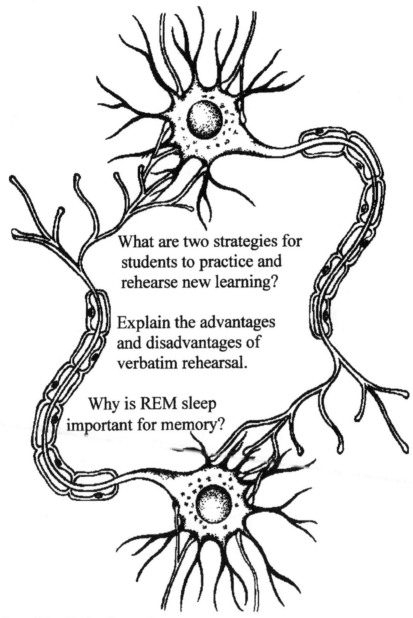

What are two strategies for students to practice and rehearse new learning?

Explain the advantages and disadvantages of verbatim rehearsal.

Why is REM sleep important for memory?

Figure 5.1. Making Connections

6

NURTURE YOUR NEURONS

There was no time for play.
This was no time for fun.
This was no time for games.
There was work to be done.

—Dr. Seuss

We are nearing the end of our journey through the brain; however, before we are finished, I would like to share a few suggestions about how to keep your brain energized and in top mental condition. Anyone who has flown in a commercial airliner can recall the flight attendant's instructions regarding cabin depressurization: "If you are required to use the oxygen mask, first take care of yourself before helping others." Although initially this may sound selfish, if you do not maintain an adequate supply of oxygen to your brain, you cannot provide assistance to those around you.

This same analogy can be applied for teachers and administrators. Before we can truly foster a brain-friendly learning environment for our students, we must first take care of ourselves. Too frequently educators become so consumed with grading papers, preparing lesson plans, and attending meetings that we neglect our personal health and welfare. To paraphrase the rhyme by Dr. Seuss: There was no time for play, fun, or games because there was work to be done. If teachers fall prey to this stressful and harmful cycle of professional overachieving, it becomes difficult to provide our students with a relaxed and intellectually challenging brain-friendly classroom.

Of course, there is no miracle memory pill or medical panacea that can transform your brain to produce photographic memory. However, there are activities and life-style strategies that will increase your chances of maintaining an efficient brain with excellent memory. The following section will provide practical suggestions to maintain a healthy brain.

STRATEGIES TO MAINTAIN A HEALTHY BRAIN

Maintain a reasonable exercise program. First, a note of caution, consult your physician before starting any exercise program. After you have gotten a "clean bill of health" from your doctor, begin doing regular physical exercise. Start with activities that you enjoy: walking, biking, playing tennis, swimming, and as your body allows, advance to more vigorous exercises. The benefits of exercise are numerous: it reduces the risk of diabetes, heart attacks, and colon cancer, and over 1,000 studies have shown that aerobic exercise can help alleviate the symptoms of mild to moderate depression (Ratey, 2001). An additional benefit of exercise is it actually stimulates the growth of new brain cells, which helps to increase your memory and enhances your ability to learn new information.

Drink water. The brain is primarily composed of cerebral spinal fluid and the main source of this fluid is water. If you do not consume an adequate amount of water, it can subtly impair your ability to think and diminish your memory capacity. Simply consuming an adequate amount of pure, clean drinking water throughout the day can help the brain function more efficiently. The following is a straightforward, unscientific formula to determine your amount of daily water consumption. First, take your weight and divide it in half. This provides an approximate amount of water in ounces that you should drink each day. For example, if you weigh 150 pounds, your recommended daily water consumption is 75 ounces. There are many factors that impact hydration levels such as stress, exercise, and ambient temperature; therefore this formula should be used only as a guide for your daily water consumption.

Proper nutrition. Maintaining proper nutrition is an important aspect of sustaining a healthy brain. Eating foods that are rich in antioxidants can help to absorb free-radicals, a harmful by-product of cell division that can interfere with the normal functions of brain cells. The following fruits and vegetables are great sources of antioxidants: prunes, raisins, blueberries, strawberries, oranges, kiwi, cauliflower, bananas, beets, spinach, and tofu (Carper, 2000). For additional dietary suggestions, visit your local health food store or bookstore.

Challenge your brain. Your brain is similar to your muscles and as the old adage goes: Use it or lose it! If you stop challenging and stimulating your brain, the neural networks will weaken and your ability to learn new information will diminish. David Snowdon (2001) conducted extensive research on nuns who belong to the School of Sisters of Notre Dame. The nuns, many of whom were living and working well into their eighties and nineties, were monitored for dementia and Alzheimer's disease. The results of the research revealed that those nuns who continually challenged their brains through stimulating work, crossword puzzles, and other intellectually provocative activities had fewer signs of memory problems or Alzheimer's disease. So, continue learning and challenging your brain—all of your life!

Surround yourself with a positive network of friends and family. The brain functions more efficiently when it is immersed in a safe and supportive environment. The daily stress of your career and personal responsibilities can take a significant toll on your health. A strong network of family and friends is an important link to good mental health.

Laugh. Laughter releases neurotransmitters and proteins in the brain that can boost your immune system, improve your mood, increase your oxygen and blood flow, and enhance your memory. Laughter is good for your body and great for your brain.

A potpourri of suggestions. The following ideas are a variety of suggestions that can stimulate your neurons and promote a healthy brain.

- learn a new hobby
- read a variety of books/magazines
- attend theatrical plays
- do mental math calculations
- learn a foreign language
- take a different direction to work
- learn to play chess
- play scrabble or other word games
- work crossword puzzles
- learn sign language
- recall old memories from trips/vacations
- perform your daily routine differently
- play a musical instrument
- keep a writing journal
- attend informative lectures
- talk with provocative people

SUMMARY

This concludes our journey of the brain and the I-CAN Model. I hope you found the information in this book to be practical and useful for your classroom. However, more importantly, I hope that you have developed a passion to learn more about brain-friendly learning, because this knowledge has the potential to transform what we do in education.

The successful schools of the future will be the ones that effectively develop instructional strategies that include what we are learning about the human brain and memory. Teachers and administrators who recognize the significance of brain research, who conscientiously keep abreast of pertinent neurological studies, and who tenaciously apply this knowledge in their classroom can positively change the course of education.

In conclusion, please remember that you have the power to actually influence and change the brain of every student in your classroom; it's truly an awesome responsibility. By embracing the principles of brain-friendly learning, we can all emulate Duncanville Independent School District's motto and become *Champions for Children.*

REFERENCES

Allen, R. (2001). Make me laugh using humor in the classroom. *Education Update, 43*(5), 1–8.

Bartzokis, G. (2001). Brain development continues into fifth decade of life. *Archives of General Psychiatry, 58*(5), 461–465.

Bluestein, J. (1995). *Mentors, masters, and Mrs. Macgregor: stories of teachers making a difference.* Deerfield Beach, Florida: Health Communications.

Carper, J. (2000). *Your miracle brain.* New York: HarperCollins.

Carter, R. (1998). *Mapping the mind.* Berkeley: University of California Press.

Caterino, M., & Polak, E. (1999). Effects of two types of activities on the performance of second- , third- , and fourth-grade students on a test of concentration. *Perceptual Motor Skills, 89*(1), 245–248.

Cranz, G. (1998). *The chair: rethinking culture, body and design.* New York: W.W. Norton.

Damasio, A. (1999). *The feelings of what happens: body and emotions in the making of consciousness.* New York: Harcourt Brace & Company.

Dennison, P., & Dennison, G. (1994). *Brain gym.* Ventura, California: Edu-Kinesthetics.

Diamond, A. (2000). Close interrelation of motor development and cognitive development and of the cerebellum and prefrontal cortex. *Child Development, 71,* 44–56.

Diamond, M., & Hopson, J. (1998). *Magic trees of the mind.* New York: Dutton.

Drubach, D. (2000). *The brain explained.* Upper Saddle River, New Jersey: Prentice-Hall, Inc.

Eliot, L. (1999). *What's going on in there? how the brain and mind develop in the first five years of life.* New York: Bantam Books.

Fahey, J. A. (2000). Water, water everywhere. *Educational Leadership, 57*(6), 60–61.

Farmer, B. (2000). In a Michigan class, music is major. *NEA Today, 18*(4), 1.

Gertz, D. (1999). *Liebman's neuroanatomy made easy and understandable* (6th ed.). Gaithersburg, Maryland: Aspen Publication.

Gilman, S., & Newman, S. (1996). *Essentials of clinical neuroanatomy and neurophysiology* (9th ed.). Philadelphia: F.A. Davis Company.

Hannaford, C. (1995). *Smart moves: why learning is not all in your head.* Arlington, Virginia: Oceans Publishers.

Hathaway, W. (1995). Effects of school lighting on physical development and school performance. *Journal of Educational Research, 88*(4), 228–242.

Hattie, J. (1992). Measuring the effects of schooling. *Australian Journal of Education, 36*(1), 5–13.

Hobson, J. A. (1999). Order from chaos. In R. Conlan (Ed.), *States of mind: new discoveries about how our brains make us who we are* (pp. 179–199). New York: John Wiley & Sons, Inc.

Holmes, T. H., & Rache, R. H. (1967). The social readjustment rating scale. *Journal of Psychosomatic Research, 2*(11), 213–218.

Howard, P. (2000). *The owner's manual for the brain* (2d ed.). Austin: Bard Press.

Jensen, E. (1995). *Brain-based learning and teaching.* Del Mar, California: Turning Point Publishing.

Jensen, E. (1998). *Teaching with the brain in mind.* San Diego: The Brain Store.

Jensen, E. (2000). *Learning with the body in mind.* San Diego: The Brain Store.

Koob, G. (1999). Corticotropin-releasing factor, norephinephrine, and stress. *Society of Biological Psychiatry, 46,* 1167–1180.

Kotulak, R. (1996). *Inside the brain.* Kansas City: Andrew McMeel.

Kuller, R., & Lindsten, C. (1992). Health and behavior of children in classrooms with and without windows. *Journal of Environmental Psychology, 12,* 305–317.

LeDoux, J. (1998). *The emotional brain.* New York: Simon & Schuster.

Ling, J., & Blades, M. (2000). The effect of nonverbal aid on preschoolers' recall for color. *Journal of Genetic Psychology, 161,* 314–324

Mesulam, M. (2000). *Principles of behavioral and cognitive neurology* (2d ed.). New York: Oxford University Press.

Marzano, R., Pickering, D., & Pollock, J. (2001). *Classroom instruction that works: research based strategies for increasing student achievement.* Reston: Association of Supervision and Curriculum Development.

Mastropieri, M., & Scruggs, T. (1989). Mnemonic instruction of learning disabled students: a field based evaluation. *Learning Disability Quarterly, 12,* 119–125.

Mastropieri, M., & Scruggs, T. (1991). *Teaching students ways to remember: strategies for learning mnemonically.* Cambridge: Brookline Books.

McAllister, R. (2001, August 22). Laughter free, available without prescription. *Kingsport Times-News,* p. C5.

McKhann, G., & Albert, M. (2002). *Keeping your brain young: the complete guide to physical and emotional health and longevity.* New York: John Wiley & Sons, Inc.

Miles, E. (1997). *Tune your brain.* New York: Penguin Putnam, Inc.

Milner, A. D., & Goodale, M. A. (1996). *The visual brain.* New York: Oxford University Press.

Milner, P. (1999). *The autonomous brain: a neural theory of attention and learning.* Mahwah, New Jersey: Lawrence Erlbaum Associates.

Olber, L., & Gjerlow, K. (1999). *Language and the brain.* United Kingdom: Cambridge University Press.

Pert, C. (1997). *Molecules of emotion.* New York: Scribner.

Ratey, J. (2000). *A user's guide to the brain.* New York: Pantheon Books.

Restak, R. (2001). *Mozart's brain and the fighter pilot.* New York: Harmony Books.

Rose, C. (1985). *Accelerated learning.* New York: Dell Publishing.

Sapolsky, R. (1998). *Why zebras don't get ulcers.* New York: Freeman.

Schacter, D., & Scarry, E. (2000). *Memory, brain and belief.* Cambridge: Harvard University Press.

Shaw, G. (2000). *Keeping Mozart in mind.* San Diego: Academic Press.

Smith, F. (1986). *Insult to intelligence. The bureaucratic invasion of our classrooms.* Portsmouth, New Hampshire: Heinemann.

Snowdon, D. (2001). *Aging with grace.* New York: Bantam Books.

Sousa, D. (1995). *How the brain learns.* Reston: National Association of Secondary School Principals.

Squire, L., & Kandel, E. (1999). *Memory from mind to molecules.* New York: Scientific American Library.

Snyder, S. (1996). *Drugs and the brain.* New York: Scientific American Library.

Vos, J. (n.d.). *An introduction to the music revolution.* Retrieved July 14, 2002, from The Learning Web website: *http://www.thelearningweb.net*

Walker, A. (2000). *Memorize in minutes: the times tables.* Prosser, Washington: Krimsten Publishing.

Wong, H. K., & Wong, R. T. (1998). *The first days of school.* Mountain View, California: Harry K. Wong Publications.

Wooten, P. (1992). *Humor as therapy for patient and caregiver in pulmonary rehabilitation: guidelines to success.* Philadelphia: J.B. Lippincott Co.

Yurgelun-Todd, D., Baird, A., & Gruber, S., et al. (1999). Functional magnetic resonance imaging of facial affect recognition in children and adolescents. *American Academy of Child and Adolescent Psychiatry, 38*(2), 195–199.

Zeki, S. (1999). *The visual image in the brain and mind.* New York: Lyons Press.

INDEX

ABOUT THE AUTHOR

Lowell W. Biller is a life-long educator and educational consultant who is passionate about brain-friendly learning. He has served students at all levels of K–12 education as a teacher and administrator and has written numerous articles on the subject of the human brain and learning. In addition, Lowell has "shadowed" neurosurgeons and medical school professors, both in the operating room and classroom, in an attempt to learn more about the fascinating field of neuroscience. He is founder of I-CAN Learning Strategies, an educational consulting business for brain-friendly learning, and is a certified Brain-Compatible Trainer by the Eric Jensen Learning Corporation. Lowell can be reached at *dbiller659@aol.com* or visit his website at: *http://www. I-CANlearningstrategies.com/.*